GARDENING BY THE SEASONS

A Collection of Articles

by Rhonda Ferree

WingSpan Press

Printed in the United States of America

Published by WingSpan Press, Livermore, CA
www.wingspanpress.com

The WingSpan name, logo and colophon are the trademarks of
WingSpan Publishing.

ISBN 978-1-59594-186-2

First edition 2007

Library of Congress Control Number 2007935514

TABLE OF CONTENTS

ACKNOWLEDGMENTS

There are many people to thank for making this book possible.

Certainly, this book and its contents would not be possible without the staff at University of Illinois Extension – Fulton County. Becky Campbell and Debbie Shelby helped immensely with their editing and column distribution skills.

The column was published weekly in the Canton Daily Ledger. Thanks to Ledger staff for diligently running my column each Saturday.

My inspiration for the columns came in many ways. The Fulton County Master Gardeners and Spoon River Garden Club members played a key role. So did family and friends, many whom I mentioned in various columns. Cindy McGrew and Jo Skoglund have been especially important friends to me as we've explored and studied the natural world together.

I must also thank Dr. David Williams at the University of Illinois for his help and advice over the years. Dr. Williams took a chance on me, hiring me as a Graduate Assistant and serving as my graduate advisor. As an informal mentor, Dave helped me become a better Extension employee and horticulturist.

The most thanks goes to my family. My husband Mark and sons, Derek and Tyler, have always supported and encouraged my professional career. My Mom and Dad (Doris and Ron Simmons) were instrumental in molding me into the person I am today, including my love of plants. My sister Lynn Miller has always been my friend and confidant, providing support in ways she didn't even know.

Finally, I would be remiss if I didn't thank my readers. I truly appreciated all the kind words about my articles. People often told me that they recognized my picture from the column and enjoyed reading the articles.

Thank you all!

PREFACE

This book is composed of horticultural columns that I wrote while with University of Illinois Extension – Fulton County in Lewistown, Illinois. A portion of proceeds from book sales will be donated to the Fulton County Extension office.

Each article was originally a weekly horticultural column that ran each Saturday in the Canton Daily Ledger in a special section titled, "Master Gardener's Corner." The column was meant to keep Fulton County home gardeners up to date on pertinent gardening topics. The Canton Daily Ledger is a daily newspaper based in Canton, Illinois that reaches about 5,800 readers.

I always tried to write articles that described gardening in a personal, fun, and easy to understand way, using personal examples as much as possible. The "Master Gardener's Corner" purpose was to provide timely and accurate horticultural information to the typical homeowner in Fulton County, Illinois. The column also publicized Extension programming and other interesting events in the county.

I am proud to say that I won several communication awards for this column. I was a state award winner in the personal column category of the communications award program for the National Association of County Agricultural Agents (NACAA) in 2001, 2002, and 2005. I was a regional finalist in 2001.

Why this book? There are many reasons, but the main one is to provide a lasting collection for my loyal readers.

Therefore, this is a collection of my favorite columns from the past eight years. Some articles were changed to remove time sensitive or event specific information, but otherwise they are intact. In organizing the articles by the season, the reader can go to specific topics or peruse articles throughout the year for gardening inspiration and information. I intend for this to be an easy read that will entertain and educate readers about various gardening topics.

I love plants and am happy to share some of that knowledge with you. You'll find more information about me in the first and last columns, found at the beginning and end of this book.

Enjoy … and happy gardening!

Rhonda Ferree

FIRST COLUMN

Help Available for All Your Plant-Related Questions!

Do you wonder why your crabapple trees are dropping so many yellow leaves this year? Or, want to know what the University of Illinois researchers think about this wet year and crop yields? Well, I am here to help answer all your plant-related questions. I have replaced Matt Montgomery as the Fulton County Extension Assistant in Horticulture/ Crops. My husband and our two boys are excited about returning to beautiful Spoon River Country and serving the nice people here.

I am a native of Fulton County-born and raised in Canton. After graduation from Canton High School, I enrolled at the University of Illinois in the Ornamental Horticulture program. Although my emphasis there was landscape horticulture, I took advantage of all the horticulture, soils, and pest classes I could fit in. During summers, I worked for the Canton Park District planting flowers, watering trees, mowing, and such.

I began my professional Horticultural career as a maintenance supervisor for Brickman Industries in the Chicago area. I ran a maintenance crew of 3-4 laborers and maintained 8-10 private and business grounds. I also worked in the estimating department for a time doing estimates for both landscape construction and maintenance. Although this was interesting work, we simply did not like living the suburban life.

After visiting with my professors from the University of Illinois, I decided to return there and pursue a Masters Degree in Horticulture. Since I have always had an interest in plants, even those growing out of place, I focused my Master's research on weeds in horticultural crops. At that time, I also started working for the Pesticide Applicator Training program where I continued full time upon graduation.

I am very proud of my work and accomplishments with the University of Illinois Pesticide Applicator Training program. My responsibilities included writing publications, conducting educational programs, and anything else related to pesticide safety education. I helped write many of the Pesticide Applicator Training manuals including Aquatics, Rights-of-Way, Private Applicator, General Standards, and Plant Management. My training responsibilities included commercial general standards training and weed training within several commercial categories. I was the publication coordinator for the team and helped coordinate many news releases, radio and television spots, and fact sheets.

The University of Illinois is a great resource of knowledge that I understand well; so if I don't know the answer, I'll sure try to find it somewhere.

GARDENING IN SPRING

Allergy-Free Gardening

Allergy-free gardens may sound like a dream to those who suffer with plant-related allergies. Unfortunately, I have been one of those allergy sufferers this spring and am apparently allergic to one of our spring flowering trees. Although it is impossible to have gardens that are completely allergy-free for all people, here are a few tips that might help.

Monitor pollen counts. Pollen counts are given on most television newscasts or are available on the internet. This week the culprits were maple, birch, and oak pollen. Use pollen counts to help plan your day, if possible. Pollen counts tend to rise early and late in the afternoon and are often lowest at midday.

Plant low pollen plants in your landscape. Plants are not equal in the amounts of pollen they release. High-allergy plants typically produce large amounts of wind-blown pollen.

Let's look at maples – some of which are severe allergy plants and others that are virtually allergy-free. For maples, it is all related to the sex of the tree. While some flowers have all parts in one flower, maple trees have either all male or all female flowers on whole trees. The male flowers have the pollen, while the female trees have the fruit. Since we often want maintenance-free landscapes and don't want to rake up fruit (maple seeds in this case), we tend to plant male plants that produce more pollen.

Let us look even closer at just Red Maples, which vary in allergenic potential. 'October Glory' and 'Red Sunset' Red

Maples are excellent choices for the landscape. Not only are they great trees with excellent fall color, but they also have no spring pollen. Conversely, the 'Autumn Spire' Red Maple is extremely allergenic in spring.

Research has shown that putting low-allergy plants in your yard is really beneficial. The closer you are to the source, the greater the chance of exposure. For example, birch trees are well known to produce allergenic airborne pollen that can travel on the wind for many miles. Still, one researcher observed that 99 percent of each birch tree's pollen falls out, lands, and sticks within 20 feet of the pollinating tree.

By the way, the more showy the flower, the less it's allergenic potential. In other words, ugly flowers are more likely to make you sneeze! It is all related to the way the flowers are pollinated: apple flowers pollinated by bees rarely cause allergy problems compared to ragweed pollen that is spread by wind.

I wish everyone an allergy-free spring!

Arbor Day Tree Ideas

National Arbor Day is Monday! Are you ready to plant a tree? Our family planted three trees on Earth Day this year: a beech, maple, and redbud. There are many different types of trees available. Consider planting something different this year; but of course make sure that it meets your site and personal needs. Here is why we planted the trees we did.

I love beech trees. They have a unique, showstopper look to them. The one I planted is a Purple European Beech (*Fagus sylvatica* 'Rivversii'). This tree has deep purple leaves that are almost black in early spring. I picked this tree because it is beautiful and will work well in my front yard. This is a huge specimen tree! Its habit is a dense oval that branches to the ground. In order to show this habit fully, it needs space. Our front yard is perfect and gives the plant plenty of room to reach its full 50-foot height and 45-foot spread.

We have many maples in our yard, including Norway maple, Crimson King Norway maple, and even silver maple. There are many great maples and I want more. Eventually, I'd like to add Sugar Maple, Amur Maple, and maybe Paperbark Maple. This year we planted a Red Maple.

Specifically, we planted October Glory Red Maple (*Acer Rubrum* 'October Glory'). It also went into the front yard (it is big), but was placed near a flowering dogwood tree that needs some shelter from a larger tree. Both trees were strategically placed to allow the best views from the house, yet to emphasize the house structure from outside. October Glory Red Maple is an oval-rounded maple that grows to about 50 foot by 50 foot. Its claim to fame is its brilliant orange to red fall color.

The third tree we planted this year was a Forest Pansy Redbud (*Cercis canadensis* 'Forest Pansy'). It was placed in a large hosta bed in the backyard to provide additional spring interest and shade for the hosta. Other trees already there include mature Scotch Pine and immature oak and hackberry.

You are all familiar with redbud, which is currently in full bloom everywhere. Forest Pansy is a purple leaf type. Flowers are more rose-purple than the regular species and open a little later. The plant also has very dark stems.

Consider planting your own tree this Arbor Day. Make sure you choose the right plant for the right place. Always plant a tree where it can reach its mature height and spread.

Coleus

Tropical plants are very popular this year. I'm planting tropical plants in one area of our yard. I planted a banana tree and crotons that I over wintered in my house, canna and elephant ear bulbs, and some Mother-in-Laws Tongue houseplant for an added tropical feel. For flower color, I planted red plume celosia. It all creates a much different atmosphere in that part of my yard.

One large area features different coleus. Coleus are prized for their colorful foliage which may combine shades of green, yellow, pink, red and maroon. New introductions of this popular annual have been selected for increased sun and heat tolerance.

Coleus come in many different types. Some reach only 1 foot tall while others are 3 feet and bushy. Sprawling types work well in hanging baskets and wall plantings and can spread up to 3 feet or more.

Most coleus grow really fast and reach their full size in one summer. Unfortunately, they are not winter hardy here. Most people treat them as annuals – replanting each year – but they can be moved indoors for the winter.

Most coleus grow best in part shade or dappled light. However, several new cultivars are available that will thrive in full, hot sun. Varieties that are not sun-tolerant will bleach and discolor in full sun. Watch the plant labels to be sure you place your plants in the right conditions.

Coleus do not like "wet feet." They must have good soil drainage. Poorly drained soils and excessive watering will damage coleus, causing stunted leaves with muddy brown scorched leaf margins.

Coleus respond very well to pinching young plants to encourage and maintain dense foliage. Coleus do flower, but many people do not like the flowers and pinch them off too.

Here are the coleus that I planted this year: 'Pineapple' with bright lime-gold and burgundy stems that seldom blooms, 'Wizard Mix' with intense colors in compact form, 'Black Magic' with mahogany purple leaves outlined in avocado scallops, and 'Sunset' with terrific russet-red foliage in a compact habit.

Coleus's brilliant foliage makes it a natural for use in flower beds or as a color accent. Coleus also grows beautifully in containers, which can be used to highlight patios, porches and garden terraces.

Container Gardens

Container gardening continues to be very popular. People with limited garden space and limited time to garden use containers. Containers also add new dimension, emphasis, and interest to existing gardens. They extend gardens to windowsills, balconies, porches, or other small paved areas.

Anything can be used as a container. Terracotta is very popular right now and has many nice uses. More specifically, weathered terracotta brings higher prices at the garden shops. (Hint: Make your own weathered terracotta by painting pots with a solution of organic manure, buttermilk, or diluted plain yogurt.) Other traditional container materials include plastic, wood, concrete, metal, and ceramic.

Have fun with containers by using unusual items as plant containers. Anything that will hold soil and provide drainage can be used as a container. Examples might include boots, baskets, tins, kid's toys, and so much more! Don't overdo these though. Overuse of unusual containers leads to a gaudy, unattractive garden.

Gardening in a container does present some challenges. Proper soil mixes are important to assure watering and fertilization is adequate. Containers dry out quickly. Increased watering frequency and mixes without soil often create a need for more fertilization in containers gardens.

You usually need to check the containers daily for moisture. When you water, water thoroughly so that the entire soil ball is moistened. Water dripping out of the drainage holes is usually a good sign that enough water has been applied. Light watering does not moisten the entire soil ball. This results in poor root growth and plant performance.

Extending the interval between watering is sometimes achieved with the use of one of the many polymers on the market. These are sold under a variety of trade names and are essentially the same material found in diapers. They are added to the soil mix and are capable of holding and retaining moisture for use by the plants when the soil is dry. They must be used carefully and as directed on the label. Improper usage can cause additional problems for your plants.

Design principles for plants and containers are fun to play with too. Use a mixture of companion plants in a container to create a desired color or texture theme. Similarly, the containers themselves can be grouped by texture, type, or color. Anything is possible.

Dandelions and Earth Day

Today is the 30th anniversary of Earth Day. On this day, take time to reflect about our world around us. You might even try to look at a small piece of our world from a completely different viewpoint. Take dandelions for example. To many people the dandelion is a weedy pest that invades our lawns; but other people find many positive attributes in the plant.

Kids love dandelions. They enjoy collecting masses of blooms to give to their mothers. As a mother, I equally enjoy receiving the clumps of yellow blooms. Tyler, my 5-year old, gives me another blossom almost every day and I love every one he gives. They don't last long, but the thought is what really matters. Kids also love the seedheads that follow flowers. Who can't remember blowing dandelions and watching them float on the breeze?

Dandelions actually have several uses including culinary, medicinal, cosmetic, and commercial. For at least 1,000 years, the dandelion has been in constant use as both a food and a medicine. Like so many plants, its origins were in the Mediterranean regions of Europe and Asia Minor.

History shows that the dandelion was brought to this country for its culinary uses. There are even books that detail how to grow this "new" crop. "About 4 pounds of seed to the acre should be allowed, sown in drills, 1 foot apart." "The yield should be 4 or 5 tons of fresh roots to the acre in the second year." Can you picture an entire field of dandelions?

Actually that is not difficult, since it is very prevalent in some grassy fields.

Dandelions are used commercially in the United States. Large quantities of the plant's leaves supply a considerable popular demand for fresh spring greens in many ethnic grocery stores and supermarkets. Additionally, dandelion roots are domestically grown for use in patent medicines and more than 100,000 pounds are imported annually to fulfill the pharmaceutical needs.

In addition to the leaves, dandelions are cooked as a potherb or infused as a tea. One source says that it's the dandelion flowers that pack a wallop! Yes the flowers are also edible. My Grandma used to fry them like mushrooms in the early spring and I enjoyed eating them.

So look at the dandelion differently this Earth Day. You might even celebrate the day with a salad of dandelion greens, followed by fried flower heads and a glass of dandelion wine. Supposedly the best dandelions are found where no lawnmower has touched them. But, of utmost importance look for a lawn that has not been sprayed if you plan to eat from it.

Easter Lilies

The popular Easter lily is the Christian symbol of purity, innocence, and chastity. But this particular lily has been popular for eons. In the Semitic world, it is the symbol of motherhood. It was the flower of Aphrodite, the Greek goddess of love, and was later the flower of Roman Goddess's Diana and Venus.

Today, the lily sold as the Easter lily is most likely the *Lilium candidum*, known by the common name of Madonna lily. It is somewhat sad to see it used only as a potted plant because it also makes a gorgeous garden plant. Do not throw out your Easter lily when it is done blooming. Instead, after your lily finishes flowering, keep it watered until the leaves turn yellow. Then, about Memorial Day you can plant your lily bulb outdoors and watch it bloom again later this summer.

The Madonna Lily bulb should be planted close to the surface of the soil, which is different from most other lilies. This year it should send up a new shoot later this summer and bloom before frost. One of my college friends planted their Easter lilies outside their church and they were in full bloom during their late summer wedding.

The bulb should overwinter here and bloom in July in subsequent years. In the garden, the flowering stem carries as many as 15 or more pure white fragrant flowers 5 inches in diameter, reaching a height of 48 inches or more.

There are many other types of true lilies available for the garden ranging in colors of white, orange, scarlet, rose, pink, or yellow. True lilies are different from day lilies in leaf and flower arrangement. True lilies have leaves going up a single stem with flowers at the top, whereas day lilies have long leaves and flower stalks coming from large clumps. Because of their singular and striking habit, true lilies are excellent as single specimens or in solid masses.

Lilies do well in full sun or partial shade. Provide fertile soil and mulch to keep the root zone cool. Drainage is very important for this species. Typically the bulbs are planted in the fall. Most lily bulbs are planted with 4 to 6 inches of soil above the top of the bulb.

Finally, should you remove the yellow stamens or not? Removing the yellow stamens inside the bloom is simply a matter of choice and aesthetics. Removal does not make the flower last longer. The only reason to remove it is for looks since as the pollen falls from the stamen it can stain the flower.

Happy Easter!

Garlic Mustard is Invading Our Woods!

As many of you know by now, I love spring wildflowers. Each year, however, my search for spring wildflowers reveals a sad new disturbance among our woodland flora. Garlic mustard,

Alliaria petiolata, is becoming a major weed among our native wildflowers!

Garlic mustard is not a weed to take lightly; if you have it, control is imperative. I have seen large expanses of this weed choke out native plants at Allerton and Lodge Parks in central Illinois. As I drive around Fulton County, garlic mustard is seen along the edges of most wooded areas.

This plant occurs most frequently in upland and floodplain forests, savannas, and along roadsides. It invades shaded areas, especially disturbed sites, and open woodland. It is capable of growing in dense shade and occasionally occurs in areas receiving full sun.

In Illinois, the plant behaves mostly as a biennial. After germinating in the spring, the plant spends its first summer and winter as a rosette of heart-shaped leaves (2-8" long) with coarse, round, irregular teeth on the margins. The following spring, the plants send up a 1-2 foot flowering stalk of small, four-petaled, white flower clusters.

The plant spreads exclusively by seed on the fur of larger animals such as deer, by flowing water, and by human activities. Seeds disperse when the seedpods burst at maturity in August. Seeds have a 20-month dormancy period and do not germinate until the second spring after ripening. Some plants produce as many as 8,000 seeds! Therefore, the goal of any garlic mustard control program is to prevent seed production until the seed bank is exhausted, usually a two to five-year period. I cannot emphasize the importance of not letting this plant go to seed!

I am able to ignore many weeds, but I always instantly pull or cut any of these growing on my property. Removal of plants by hand pulling is effective if the root is removed. If the stem snaps off from the root crown of a non-flowering plant, the plant may resprout.

The Nature Conservancy has successfully controlled or eliminated this plant from several sites by a combination of spring burning, hand-pulling, and cutting flowering stems with a scythe.

Spot application of Roundup (a formulation of glyphosate)

to the foliage of individual plants is effective during spring and fall when most native vegetation is dormant but garlic mustard remains green.

Foundation Plants

Last weekend I started redesigning the front of my house. It currently has old, overgrown yews all around the house foundation and I am ready for a change. Foundation plantings are the combination of plants around the front door, the front corners, and a transition area that joins them.

Plants along the front of a house serve many purposes. A properly designed front landscape can greatly enhance the appearance and market value of your property. Use plants to blend the structure of the house with the general surroundings so that the house looks natural on its site.

To get you started, stand in front of your house and draw a rough sketch that shows the front door, windows, and roof lines. Then draw a "V" from each corner eave down to the front door. The "V" serves as guidelines for plant heights along the front of the house. The tallest plants at the ends of the "V" should be no taller than two-thirds the height of the corners of the house. Select plants for the entrance that don't become too large.

Think of your front door as the center of interest and focal point. The entrance planting should help direct attention to the door. Use plants with year-round interest, because they are seen closely and many times.

Do not think you have to put plants all the way across the foundation. The main idea is to soften the homes features, not camouflage. Only if this space is exceptionally long may some plants be used to break the long line. Avoid long rows of the same type of plant to fill these areas. In some situations a bed of groundcover or mulch may be all that is necessary to tie the entrance planting and corner plantings together and also make maintenance and mowing easier.

Don't locate plants other than groundcovers within 1 1/2 feet of the foundation where the soil is often too dry for good plant growth. Plants should be far enough from the house to avoid growing against the house and to maintain good air circulation. For spreading shrubs, allow for width equal to the eventual height. Good spacing is important to prevent later crowding and excess pruning.

Unfortunately, not all homes and lots fit the situation described here. Since houses come in all shapes and sizes, there is no "cookbook" recipe for landscaping. Every situation is unique and different. Regardless of your situation, remember these key points: the house is the focal point, focus on the front door, and soften architectural features so that the house blends in with its surroundings.

Fragrant Gardens

I've enjoyed cut lilacs on my kitchen table all week. The fragrance is heavenly every time I walk into the kitchen. Adding fragrance to a garden excites our senses and adds another dimension to the gardening experience. Here are several examples to try in your garden.

Lilacs come in many types, including common lilac (*Syringa vulgaris*), dwarf lilacs (*S. meyeri* and *patula*) and even tree lilacs (*S. reticulata*). With careful selection you can find plants with good mildew resistance in the exact color, size, and degree of fragrance you desire. Flowers are typically lavender or white in color.

Honeysuckle shrubs have very fragrant flowers in the spring. There are many types of honeysuckle available and careful selection is important, as many can become quite weedy. The most fragrant is probably the winter honeysuckle (*Lonicera fragrantissima*). It has powerful fragrance that perfumes an entire garden in March and April.

One of the most fragrant shrubs is the Koreanspice Viburnum (*Viburnum carlesii*). It has a spicy-sweet fragrance that is different from the flowery smells of honeysuckle and lilac. I have this plant next to my patio so I can enjoy the smells while resting there. This shrub grows 4 to 8 feet high and wide, although a compact version is available, too. Flowers are 2- to 3-inch diameter pinkish-white balls.

Other shrubs with strong fragrance include other viburnums, roses, some rhododendrons, and fothergilla. Fothergilla is listed as having a honey scent. Privet (*Ligustrum* sp.) is sometimes described as "sickeningly sweet."

In addition to woody plants there are many flowers and groundcovers with fragrant flowers or foliage. Many examples include dianthus, hosta, iris, lavender, mint, peony, and violet, to name a few.

One of my favorite flowers is Lily of the Valley (*Convallaria majalis*). It is a groundcover with fragrant flowers that grow best in a shady site. Flowers are white (or pink) and appear like small bells growing up a stem. Just a few of these in an arrangement will fill a room with a fragrant smell. Once established, they can become aggressive, so plant them where you want them.

Finally, no fragrant garden is complete without peony (*Paeonia* hybrids). These shrub-shaped perennial plants have 3 to 6 inch flowers of various colors. According to one source, the peony fragrance can by very sweet and overwhelmingly strong.

Excite more of your senses this year by adding fragrance to your garden. Your nose will thank you!

Fruit Trees

I've had many calls recently concerning fruit trees. Questions have included how to prune for good fruit production, when and what to spray for proper pest management, and why trees fail to bear. Fruit trees are a great asset to the home garden, but they do require some homework. Proper planting, pruning, fertilizing, and fruit-thinning are essential for fruit production and are important pest management practices as well.

The proper way to prune (and train) a fruit tree really depends on the tree itself. Typically we prune fruit trees annually to keep them short and open. For semi-dwarf apple and pear, a standard central leader system is recommended compared to an open center system used on peach and nectarine trees. It is imperative to start proper pruning and training in the tree's first year. Reviving old fruit trees is very difficult, if not sometimes impossible. Well-pruned trees are less susceptible to several diseases and are easier to spray.

Many different pests attack tree fruits. The best way to control pests is to start by planting the right tree. Researchers and breeders have developed many cultivars with disease resistance to fruit tree diseases such as apple scab, powdery mildew, cedar apple rust, and fire blight.

Most homeowners prefer to use a multipurpose fruit spray. These mixes usually contain one or two insecticides, one or two fungicides, and rarely a miticide. Alternative insecticides that are approved for use on fruits in organic production and are available to homeowners include insecticidal soap and *Bt* product. Follow the product label explicitly! The label is the law. Following it to the tee ensures food safety and pest management. If damage-free fruit is your goal, do not skip sprays. Depending on the crop, sprays may be needed on a 7 to 14 day schedule.

Finally, I am often asked why a tree will not bear. There are several things that influence tree fruit production, but the four major factors are the normal bearing age for that variety, tree health, climate, and pollination. Dwarf trees typically bear in 2-4 years compared to 3-5 years for most standards. Tree health is necessary to promote good fruiting. Weak or diseased trees produce poor quality fruit or no fruit at all. Climate and weather play a big role. Resistance to cold temperatures varies among types of fruits. The most sensitive are apricots and sweet cherries, followed by peaches, the moderately sensitive plums, pears, and sour cherries, and the hardy apples.

Key to fruit production is an understanding of how the tree pollinates. Some trees must be pollinated by another tree to produce fruit. Check the tree tag or catalog carefully when buying fruit trees to be sure you have the proper "mix".

Garden Structures

Do you have a porch or a veranda? Garden structures are an important part of the garden, but terms and definitions can be confusing. Here is a listing of popular garden structures with their definitions.

Pergola – Last year we built a pergola at the back of our house. A pergola is an open structure, usually on regularly spaced posts or columns with a lattice or open frame top. This garden structure adds shade to a walk or passageway and is usually covered by climbing plants.

Arbor – Simply put, an arbor is a simple, less extensive pergola. Arbors are light, open structures formed from plants that twine together to form an arch overhead or arbors are formed from a latticework frame covered with plants. Arbors can also be metal or wooden structures in the shape of an arch.

Bower – Another form of an arbor is a bower. A bower is typically wider than an arbor and provides an intimate alcove where you can sit, relax, and contemplate.

Trellis – This is even simpler than an arbor. It is a structure of open latticework, especially one used as a support for vines and other creeping plants. A trellis is often freestanding and does not form an arch.

Veranda – This is a porch or balcony that extends along the outside of a building. Verandas are usually roofed and partly enclosed. We usually think of a veranda as part of elegant and expensive architecture.

Porch – We all know what a porch is. It is a covered platform at an entrance to a building that usually has a separate roof. Sitting on a swing under the covered porch brings back memories of cool summer evenings.

Portico - A porch or walkway with a roof supported by columns, often leading to the entrance of a building.

Gazebo –A gazebo is a small structure, usually roofed and

open-sided. Gazebos are often located in gardens or parks where there is a nice view or focal point. I have a small gazebo in another section of my yard. It has a small water garden in front of it and a butterfly garden around it.

Solarium — A sun house or solarium is a building or room designed to receive maximum sunlight. Sometimes an enclosed porch is called a sunroom.

I'm sure you can think of other garden structure terms too. Regardless of the official name, garden structures add a great dimension to any garden.

Herb Gardens

Herbs are easy to grow, beautiful, fun, and rewarding to use. Most of them are as easy to grow as common vegetables. Whether you use them in formal herb gardens or interplanted with your vegetables or landscaping, you can always find space in a garden for a few herbs.

Botanically speaking, an herb is any plant that dies back to the root each year. But by horticultural or culinary definition, an herb is a plant that is used as an ingredient for health, flavor, or fragrance. Most of us routinely use herbs when cooking. Even an average cook knows how to use sage when stuffing the Thanksgiving turkey, chives on a baked potato, and garlic on garlic bread. But, you haven't really tasted any of these dishes until they are made with fresh herbs directly from the garden. My Grandma Kinsel always insisted that stuffing just wasn't stuffing without "fresh" sage!

It is still not too late to consider herbs for your garden this year. For those of you without a garden, many herbs grow well indoors, too. Here are a few more facts about herbs.

Culinary experts classify herbs into two groups: robust herbs and fine herbs. Robust herbs are added while food is being prepared or cooked, while fine herbs are eaten uncooked in salads or sprinkled over a cooked dish.

Use less dried product by weight or volume, but experiment with fresh herbs to adjust quantities.

Italian seasonings include such herbs as basil, oregano, fennel, flat-leaf parsley, and garlic (or garlic chives).

Mexican assortments would contain cilantro (coriander), basil, Chile peppers, and tomatillo.

Herbs are available as seed or transplants. All the annual herbs come easily from seed, but at this late date plants would be better. Perennial plants such as rosemary, thyme, and sage are most successful when grown from plants or rooted cuttings. Once started, herbs experience relatively few problems from insects or diseases. Many of the strong odors and tastes of herbs have evolved to ward off or discourage insects.

Horticultural Grilling

What do plants have to do with grilling – other than eating vegetables? Well, great chefs use many "tricks" to get just the right taste from their grill and many of those tricks involve plants.

First, chefs swear by certain types of wood chips to smoke their meat (or vegetables) on the grill. You'll find the chips in hardware and homes stores. They include oak, mesquite and hickory for a bold taste, and fruit woods and vines for lighter flavor. Avoid soft woods, such as pine, which give off a not-so-tasty resin.

The wood is usually soaked in water before cooking begins, so it burns more slowly and creates a moist, penetrating smoke. Although you can use a fire made solely of the flavoring wood, most people build a bed of coals with wood or charcoal, and add pieces of smoke wood.

Some chefs will use smoke alone, while others use smoke in combinations with the marinades and other techniques before cooking that enhance the taste of smoked foods. For fun, try your meals both ways and see which you like best. To start, toss a few chips on the coals while cooking burgers.

Learn to pair woods to particular meals. For pheasant, chicken or light-flavored fish, for example, consider the sweeter tastes of fruit woods such as cherry or apple. Stronger flavored foods, such as beef, pork or salmon, benefit from the assertiveness of hickory and mesquite.

Second is the chef's secret marinade, mop, or rub recipe, which add flavor to meats.

Rubs are blends of dried herbs and spices that flavor the exterior of meat as it cooks.

Marinades, made with herbs, spices and an acidic liquid such as wine vinegar or lemon juice, enhance the flavor of meats.

A mop is a sauce that keeps the rubbed meat from drying while it is smoke-cooked. A mop can be anything from a bottle of your favorite barbecue sauce diluted with vinegar to a rub that you've held aside and combined with beer or another liquid.

Get outdoors and grill with your family. Your taste buds will thank you!

Magnolias

Last weekend I bought two new magnolias to plant in the front of my house. One is white and one is yellow. They are part of my front foundation planting renovation.

Worldwide, there are about 80 different types of magnolias, although only 3 to 4 do well in central Illinois. Magnolias can grow as large trees or in shrub form. They are usually grown for their spectacular spring flowers. Most have showy, fragrant flowers that are white, pink, purple, green, or yellow. The flowers are followed by showy red or pink fruits displaying red, orange, or pink seeds.

The magnolias that grow best here are the Saucer, Star, and Cucumber. As with all plants, each of these has been manipulated by the nursery trade into really great cultivars with specific characteristics.

The Saucer Magnolia (*Magnolia* x *soulangiana*) is one of the most popular magnolias in the landscape. It is known for its showy pinkish purple saucer-like flowers. The regular Saucer Magnolia grows 20 to 30 feet tall by 20 to 30 feet wide in a rounded to broad-rounded form. It is often low branching and multi-stemmed. There are many cultivars of this hybrid species.

My yellow magnolia is a form of the Cucumbertree Magnolia (*Magnolia acuminata*) called 'Butterflies'. Recently, plant breeders have been successful in creating really outstanding yellow magnolias. The Butterfly Magnolia has probably the deepest darkest yellow of the yellow magnolias. The 5" across deep yellow flowers appear at a much earlier age than other yellow selections, as young as three years old rather than 6-7 years for the 'Elizabeth' & 'Yellow Lantern'. The Butterfly Magnolia also only reaches 20' tall and is more upright in habit, compared to 50 to 80 foot rounded form of the straight Cucumbertree.

My white magnolia is a Royal Star (*Magnolia stellata* 'Royal Star'). The Royal Star is a beautiful white-flowered selection with four to five-inch flowers that have 25-30 strap-like tepals. This is a very common star magnolia in the trade. It grows 15-20' high in a rounded to slightly broad-rounded form.

All the magnolias listed here are hardy in central Illinois. All prefer full sun and well-drained soil. They are not always tolerant of extreme drought or wetness. The main problem all magnolias encounter here is the flower's cold sensitivity. Flowers that look stunning during the day can become a mass of limp brown petals with just one cold evening. Still the often short-lived flowers are well worth a quick glimpse of their beauty.

The Meaning of Flowers

Next week is Valentine's Day. Do you have flowers ordered for your loved one? Flowers are a great way to communicate your love and affection. Over the years, flowers have developed meaning and are known as a way to convey a special message.

Flowers can represent everything from friendship to

true love. Chrysanthemums show friendship. Gardenias represent secret love. Lilies are a traditional wedding flower and mean chastity, innocence, and purity. Give a primrose to say, "I can't live without you." Another popular wedding bouquet flower is the stephanotis to show happiness in marriage. Tulips are given to the perfect lover and more specifically a red tulip declares your love. Finally, orchids are commonly given as corsages to show love and beauty.

But no other flower shows more meaning than a rose. According to the Rose Information Bureau, each rose color has a special meaning. All roses symbolize love, but certain colors of roses can take on special meanings. What's more, when several colors in various stages of bloom are combined in one arrangement, your floral bouquet can speak a whole sentence instead of just one thought. Here are some of the most widely accepted meanings for different rose colors, blooms, and arrangements:

- Red roses show love, respect, or courage
- Yellow roses represent joy, gladness, or freedom
- Pink/peach roses exude gratitude, appreciation, admiration or sympathy
- White roses demonstrate reverence, purity, secrecy
- Two roses joined together display engagement
- Red and white roses together prove unity

Additionally rosebuds say, "You are young and beautiful." A single rose stands for simplicity. In full bloom, it means "I love you" or "I love you still," and a bouquet of roses in full bloom signifies gratitude.

If you receive fresh flowers for Valentine's Day, here are some tips to ensure the longest vase life. Don't let your flowers get thirsty or hungry. Add water containing floral food to the vase every day. The best flower food can be obtained from your floral retailer.

Once the flowers are past their prime, discard them or make the memory last. Roses, for example, can be made into many lasting memories. Make a rose potpourri out of your rose petals. Press and dry the flowers for your memory book. Dry the roses upside down and then run string through individual heads to create a garland. The uses of flowers are endless.

Happy Valentine's Day everyone!

Mother's Day

Don't forget your special Mom on Mother's Day tomorrow! If you haven't bought something special for her yet, consider these ideas. You can be sure I'll get my Mom (Doris Simmons) a special horticultural gift for Mother's Day.

A gift of fresh flowers always says, "I love you!" Many beautiful bouquets are available at the local florist. Options might include sending all cut flowers, a live plant, a fun balloon arrangement, or any combination of these. To keep cut flowers fresh longer, be sure to add floral preservative and keep watered.

For some it is family tradition to give mother a new rose bush every year to add to the rose garden. The All-America Rose Selection (AARS) winners for 2003 are Hot Cocoa, Whisper, Cherry Parfait, and Eureka. According to the AARS website (www.rose.org) these four roses with "dazzling and unique colors are a great additions to any garden." "They add great vigor, wonderful form and disease-resistance and even an inexperienced gardener will be able to quickly establish a showplace with these nationally AARS tested roses."

I commonly give my Mother-in-Law (Barbara Bohanan) a hanging basket for Mother's Day. Hanging baskets have increased in popularity for many years and include a variety of plant types. Baskets are available with ferns, annual flowers, seasonal plants, and other interesting hanging plants. Remember to use a nice basket to display the plant in, not just white plastic with a plastic hanger.

There are many new annuals on the market now. Consider giving your mother a sampling of these new plants to try. Million Bells (*Calibrachoa* sp.) looks like a small petunia and works well in containers. Licorice Plant (*Helichrysum petiolare*) is a foliage plant with gray-green to silver leaves that spreads several feet. Fanflower (*Scaevola aemula*) has unique ½-inch fan-shaped flowers in violet or white on 6-inch trailing stems. There are so many more examples such as lotus vine, treasure flower, butter daisy, and more!

In recent years there has been a revolution in garden products and décor. These include patio decorations, specialty tools, garden books, and even everyday practical items such as gloves, buckets, rakes, and trowels. Additionally, everyone loves collectibles – or knows someone who does. That is why garden centers often feature Boyd's Bears, Department 56 villages, and other collectable lines.

Many other horticultural gift ideas come to mind including garden center gift certificates, garden statuary, flats of perennials, a new tree, bird feeders, and so much more! Remember your Mother this year with a horticultural inspired gift.

Poppies

Poppies are one of my favorite flowers. I am not sure why, but I have a fascination with poppies. I collect antique Hall china in the orange poppy pattern and have my kitchen decorated in poppies. Of course, I also plant poppies in my garden.

This year we put in a "Wizard of Oz" garden, complete with a yellow brick road, characters, and, of course, poppies to make them sleep. Actually the poppy name was derived from *popig*, which was an Anglo-Saxon term for sleep, since the seeds from certain species were used to make a drink to induce sleepiness.

The Oriental poppy (*Papaver orientale*) is the largest and most eye-catching of the poppies. It grows 18-36 inches tall and blooms in early summer. The single flowers are orange, scarlet, pink, or white blooms with dark centers. There are many different varieties available including 'Pizzicato' that produces up to 20 huge flowers per plant and the dwarf scarlet one called "Dwarf Allegro'.

The foliage of Oriental poppy dies after flowering and leaves open spaces in the garden for the rest of the season. Use other plants around the poppy to conceal the dying foliage or vacant space. I've had good success using Baby's Breath (*Gypsophila paniculata*) and Hibiscus. Remember that poppies do best if left undisturbed. The Oriental poppy can be started by dividing old clumps or by sowing seed. Plants will not bloom until the 2nd year.

The annual-type poppies are usually grown as annuals here, although many are actually short-lived perennials. Regardless, we usually reseed or replant these each year. These poppies have a much longer bloom time than Oriental poppies. The foliage does not die back and we get flowers each year. Here are some good examples.

The Shirley poppy is a nice double poppy (*Papaver rhoeas*). The 'Angels Choir' variety is 18 to 24 inches tall with old-rose colors of pinks, whites, and reds. The 'Mother of Pearl' plants are covered in 3-inch blooms in delicate shades of soft blue, lilac, pink, white, lavender, and peach.

Finally, consider adding the California Poppy to your collection. Although in the poppy family, this is not a true poppy. The California Poppy (*Eschscholzia californica*) will flower all summer at a height of 12 to 15 inches. The ¾ to 2 ½ inch flowers are usually deep orange to pale yellow. Other colors available are bronze, scarlet, rose, or white. The 'Thai Silk Mixed' variety includes all the colors. The California Poppy will bloom in 45 to 60 days from seed and plants often self-sow themselves the next year.

Prairifire Crabapple & Amelanchiers

Hard to believe it has been a week already since the Fulton County Gardeners' Big Day. Although the day started out snowy, it certainly was a big day for gardeners in Fulton County. The day was filled with educational seminars, informational vendors, and camaraderie among area gardeners. Thank you all who attended and to University of

Illinois Master Gardeners for helping make the day better for us all!

Most of the day's activities took place in Spoon River College's cafeteria. This room has windows along one entire wall looking out onto the nearby native woods and several nice planters. Recently the college replaced some trees in this area. They asked for my recommendation and I suggested several small ornamental trees including the 'Prairifire' crabapple and the Serviceberry (*Amelanchier arborea*), which they recently planted there. These are two of my favorite smaller trees, but the 'Prairifire' (or 'Prairie Fire') deserves special attention.

Crabapples are beautiful flowering trees in the spring, but many develop apple scab or other diseases that make them unsightly later in the season. Apple scab is particularly bad in years with a wet, cool spring. One of the best ways to deal with this disease is to plant disease-resistant trees. The 'Prairifire' is an excellent example.

'Prairifire' was developed at the University of Illinois by Professor D. F. Dayton and was introduced into the trade in 1982. In 1996, the Iowa Nursery and Landscape Association named it "Tree of the Year". According to their press release, "an outstanding crabapple selection 'Prairifire' has magnificent floral and fruit display, excellent disease resistance, and unusual leaf coloration in spring and fall."

Prairifire is an upright-to-rounded tree that reaches about 20 feet wide and tall. The young leaves are red-maroon, maturing to deep green and changing to an excellent red-orange in the fall. The foliage is completely disease resistant. Flowers start out as red-purple to crimson buds that open to vivid red-purple single flowers. This tree produces masses of flowers, even at a young age. Some consider it one of the best red-flowering crabapples.

Flowers are followed by deep purple-red (1/2 inch diameter) fruit that persists into March, if not eaten by the birds. The fruit is especially attractive in October and

November. Best of all, the fruit does not drop from the tree and thus is not a high maintenance tree.

Consider the 'Prairifire' when selecting your new crabapple.

Purchasing Trees and Shrubs

Today is Gardeners' Big Day at Spoon River College from 10:00 a.m. to 3:00 p.m. I hope to see many of you there. If you haven't preregistered, walk-ins are welcome. One timely topic for today is *Tree Selection and Planting* taught by John Taylor, University of Illinois Extension Master Gardener.

Trees and shrubs are popping up at retail sales areas all around town. Retailers sell a myriad of plants in a variety of packages or market forms. The purchasing of woody plants requires consumers to make choices.

The most important choice is what type of plant to buy. Consider many factors when making this choice, as it is critical. Consider shade versus sun, soil conditions, insect and disease resistance, seasonal features, and more. Beyond this, consumers must also decide which market form or plant package to purchase. Trees and shrubs are available as bareroot, balled and burlapped, container-grown, packaged, and mechanically transplanted plants.

The most commonly sold plants are container-grown in a pot or some other type of container. Retailers like these plants because they facilitate cash and carry sales and are cleaner to transport. They are also easy to plant and care for. Because they were grown in the container, these plants have their entire root system present. Beware of root-bound container plants, especially those with roots that circle around the inside of the container. Roots that circle could cause major damage to plants later in life.

Bareroot plants do not have soil around their root system, but are usually wrapped in moist sawdust or peatmoss. Packaged plants (such as roses) are actually bareroot too. These plants are sold in dormant (without leaves) form in the early spring. Before purchasing bareroot plants, inspect them to make sure that their stems and roots have normal color and texture. Beware of plants that have either soft, mushy roots or roots that have a gray mold growing on them.

Balled and burlapped plants are the traditional market form of woody plants. This method of plant packaging involves the digging of a plant with a ball of soil around the plant's root system. The soil is held in place by a piece of burlap and sometimes a wire cage. Important: remove any twine around the tree trunk before planting these plants!

Mechanically transplanted trees allow movement of very large trees directly into the homeowner's yard using a tree spade. Although more expensive, this method provides consumers with the opportunity for larger trees and thus "instant" landscapes.

Buy and plant a tree this year. It will provide you and future generations with years of enjoyment!

Rhubarb

I love rhubarb! I like it raw and I like it prepared many different ways. Last weekend I fixed a great rhubarb crisp and we ate the whole pan in one sitting!

Rhubarb is also known as the pie plant. It is a very hardy perennial garden vegetable that grows extremely well here. Although considered a vegetable, rhubarb is used as a fruit in pies, tarts, cakes, and sauces.

Rhubarb is available in either red or green stalk varieties. A popular green stalk one is Victoria. More is available in red including Canada Red with long, thick, extra sweet stalks, Cherry Red with red in and out, Crimson Red that is tall and plump, and MacDonald with tender skin and brilliant red color.

If you want to start rhubarb, here are some tips. Plant enough for your family. A half-dozen plants should provide enough rhubarb for most families. Plant or divide rhubarb roots in early spring when the plants are still dormant for best results. You can move small plants now, but don't wait much longer.

Place roots with the crown bud 2 inches below the surface of the soil. Space the roots 36 to 48 inches apart in rows 3 to 4 feet apart. Good drainage is essential. Water new plants properly and keep weeded. Rhubarb doesn't need much additional care once established. If you want to fertilize, use a complete garden fertilizer such as 12-12-12 granules before growth begins in the spring. An application of manure or compost is beneficial in late fall or early winter. Do not cover the crowns.

Harvest requires a few rules of thumb. Never harvest rhubarb during the first year of planting or too late in the fall. The plants need upper growth to build up healthy and vigorous to make it through the winter. Stalks may be harvested for 1 or 2 weeks during the second year. By the third year, you should get a full harvest of 8 to 10 weeks.

If seedstalks and flowers develop during the spring and summer, cut them from the base of the plant. This will assure the plants put energy into more stalks and not flowers. Leafstalks are the highest quality in early spring, but can be harvested through mid-summer.

Finally, yes, rhubarb can be toxic. In fact the leaves of rhubarb are extremely poisonous. They contain large amounts of oxalic acid and should not be eaten. Also, do not feed rhubarb leaves to animals. Rhubarb stalks (stems) are safe to eat, unless the plants are severely frozen. If rhubarb leaves freeze and leafstalks are "mushy" the oxalic acid may have migrated from the leaf blades to the stems. Additionally, frozen leafstalks have poor texture and flavor and should not be eaten.

Rose Selection

Everyone loves roses. We love to receive roses and grow our own in the flower garden. A key to successful rose gardens is selection.

Buy your rose plants from reputable sources such as local nurseries, garden centers, retail stores, or mail-order companies. Choose top quality, No.1 grade plants that have been well maintained. It is best to have at least three large canes, and bulky, fibrous root systems that have not been allowed to dry out. The prepackaged dormant plants should be displayed with their roots in a moisture-holding material such as wood shavings or sphagnum moss. Generally speaking, avoid "bargain" roses and get a guarantee.

There are many different types, kinds, and varieties of roses. This can be confusing, but basically, roses are separated into two main classes--bush roses and climbing roses. The bush roses are grouped into types according to their flowering habit, winter hardiness, and other traits and include hybrid tea, floribunda, wild, old-fashioned, and the new carpet roses. The most commonly grown rose is the hybrid tea.

For help in deciding which of the many varieties of roses to buy, consult catalogs, rose societies, the many rose web sites, or choose a winner. All-America Rose Selections (AARS) chooses winners each year.

The 2001 AARS winners are Glowing Peace™, Sun Sprinkles™ and Marmalade Skies™. Glowing Peace is a rose with large, round buds that open to reveal full, 3-inch blooms featuring yellow and cantaloupe orange blended petals. Deep, glossy green foliage serves as a backdrop for the blooms and gives way to burgundy fall color. Glowing Peace, a round, bushy grandiflora, grows to 4 feet by 3 feet and is resistant to disease.

Sun Sprinkles is only the fifth miniature ever to win AARS honors. This disease resistant rose produces bright yellow blooms set against a backdrop of petite, dark green, glossy foliage. Its high, pointed oval buds spiral open to reveal 2-inch, petite, double blooms with a moderate spicy fragrance with overtones of musk. Upright and rounded, Sun Sprinkles will grow to 18 to 24 inches. Miniatures are among the most versatile of rose classes, ideal for lining walkways, growing in containers, and accenting formal rose beds.

Marmalade Skies has brilliant tangerine orange blooms from beginning to end of the blooming season. Healthy, medium olive green satiny foliage provides the perfect backdrop for the constant show of color. The floribunda produces clusters of 5 to 8 blooms—a complete bouquet—on each strong stem. Oblong buds open to reveal 2½ to 3 inch double blooms with 17 to 25 petals. This compact, round plant grows to 3 feet by 3 feet, making it the perfect rose for a hedge or a stellar addition to any existing rose bed.

Spring Lawncare

I'm already starting to get some calls about lawncare this spring. Many people are anxious to begin spring gardening and lawncare activities. What lawncare activities should we do in spring?

The key to a great lawn starts with proper turfgrass variety selection along with proper lawncare management. Well-maintained healthy turf is competitive to weeds, insects, and disease. At times, weeds do get out of control and chemical control is considered to keep weed growth at tolerable levels. Two different types of lawn weeds are targeted in the spring: annual grasses and broadleaves.

Annual grassy weeds such as crabgrass, goosegrass, barnyardgrass, fall panicum, and yellow foxtail are more tolerant of wet or compacted soils or shade than are turfgrasses. Altering the growing environment to favor the turfgrass can reduce the weed problem. If chemical control is required, timing is very important, as the weed killer should be applied before the annual grass emerges from the soil. Crabgrass will germinate when soil temperatures are greater than 55° to 60°F for 7-10 consecutive days.

The soil temperature this week in Lewistown was 45°F. My guess is that applications can begin in the next 2-4 weeks. Many preemergence herbicides are available in combination with lawn fertilizer, so if you prefer, spring fertilization can be done at the same time.

Broadleaf weed problems in lawns include dandelions, plantains, and Creeping Charlie (ground ivy). Pulling by hand is one option for control; be sure to get as much of the root system as possible. If you choose to use chemical control, there are a number of broadleaf weed herbicides available for use on lawns. Spring is a good time for these applications since the actively growing weeds take up more herbicide. Typically a two or three-way combination product is best, which includes 2,4-D, mecoprop or MCPP, or dicamba. Please be very careful with these products, as drift injury to nearby plants is a real problem. Follow labels carefully!

Perennial grassy weeds such as nimblewill, quackgrass, and tall fescue are difficult to control. Handpulling is an option, though a time consuming one. The only other option is to kill the entire area with Roundup and re-seed. Overseeding and new lawn establishment should take place in April or early May. If you can wait, late summer is a better time to start new grass seed.

If you don't use a weed and feed product in March/ April, the ideal times to fertilize lawns are near Mother's Day, Labor Day, and Halloween. The University of Illinois recommends one pound of nitrogen for every 1,000 square feet of lawn. Then be ready to mow, mow, mow, as the fertilizer will really make it grow!

Spring Wildflowers

Spring walks in the woods are very enjoyable. Many of us look for morel mushrooms, but there is much more to see at the same time. Woodland wildflowers are beautiful and a welcome sign of spring.

A common woodland wildflower is the spring beauty (*Claytonia virginica*). This is a low plant with loose clusters of pink or whitish flowers, striped with dark pink. The flowers are ½ - ¾ inch wide with five petals. Leaves are long, linear and grass-like. These flowers bloom from March to May in moist woods and clearings. This spring perennial is spectacular in large patches and grows from an underground tuber like a small potato. At my former residence near Champaign, I had beautiful large patches of these across my lawn.

A more noticeable native wildflower is Virginia Bluebell (*Mertensia virginica*). This 8-24 inch erect plant has smooth gray-green leaves and nodding clusters of light blue trumpet-shaped flowers. The individual flowers start as pink buds and open to about 1 inch long. Virginia bluebells flower from March to June in moist woods and is also a popular shade garden plant. Grown in masses, this flower is hard to miss.

There are several flowers from the poppy family making a show right now: Dutchman's Breeches (*Dicentra cucullaria*), Corydalis (*Corydalis* sp.), and Bloodroot (*Sanguinaria canadensis*). Dutchman's Breeches and Corydalis have delicate, fern-like leaves and grow to about a foot tall. Dutchman's Breeches are more common. The name comes from the clusters of fragrant, white, pantaloon-shaped flowers. Corydalis flowers are pink or yellow, tubular, and not really very showy. Bloodroot has a solitary white flower, with a golden-orange center that grows beside a lobed leaf. Roots and stems have an acrid red-orange juice, thus the name Bloodroot. It lasts for a short time and may be hard to find now.

Two more woodland flowers you are sure to see soon are wild blue phlox and wild geranium. Wild blue phlox (*Phlox divaricata*) has loose clusters of slightly fragrant light blue flowers above creeping oval leaves. Also called Wild Sweet William, it will bloom from April to June. I remember seeing these as a child while walking the woods with my dad. Wild geranium (*Geranium maculatum*) is easily recognized by its typical geranium leaves and loose clusters of lavender flowers. It grows 1-2 foot tall and is found from April to June.

These are just a few of the flowers to look for while exploring our woodlands this spring. Pick the morel mushrooms, but please leave the wildflowers. Although the ones mentioned here are numerous, some of our wildflowers are becoming rare. Leaving them assures they'll remain for others to see in the future.

Vegetable Plantings

The focus of the April Spoon River Garden Club meeting was vegetable gardens. Barney Barnard was the enthusiastic speaker who motivated attendees to grow their own gardens. Mr. Barnard emphasized that home gardening is an interesting and rewarding hobby in which the entire family can become involved.

How early you can plant depends upon the hardiness of the vegetables and is often ranked around an average frost-free date. Our average frost-free date is April 22 meaning that our last spring frost has occurred by this date about half the time over the last 30 years. Our actual frost-free date varies 2 weeks or more in either direction.

Vegetables are classified as very hardy, frost-tolerant, tender, and warm loving, according to their ability to withstand freezes, cold temperatures, or heat. We usually put vegetables into two main groups: cool-season and warm-season.

Very hardy and frost-tolerant vegetables are considered cool-season vegetables. These are for early spring planting and are usually already planted by now. Very hardy vegetables withstand freezing temperatures and hard frosts without injury and are usually planted between March 25 and April 10. Very hardy vegetables include onions, peas, potato, turnip, broccoli, and rhubarb. Frost tolerant vegetables are typically planted from April 10 –25 and can withstand light frosts. These include beet, carrot, radish, and cauliflower.

Warm-season vegetables are for late spring planting and are either tender or warm loving. Tender vegetables are typically planted between April 25 and May 10. They are injured or killed by frost and their seeds do not germinate well in cold soil. These vegetables include snap beans, sweet corn, squash, and tomato. Warm-loving vegetables are intolerant of frost and cold and are typically planted between May 10 and June 1. These include lima beans, cucumber, muskmelon, okra, pumpkin, watermelon, squash, eggplant, and pepper.

Mr. Barnard said our Extension publication *Vegetable Gardening in the Midwest* (C1331) is "one of the best." This complete, accurate, and easy-to-use guide discusses growing more than 40 vegetables and 35 herbs under Midwest conditions. Information included was gleaned from years of research on growing conditions and vegetable varieties in the trial gardens at the University of Illinois.

Whether you have a large garden or just a couple tomato plants, share it with the whole family. My sons absolutely had a ball planting our potatoes and onions this year. Gardening provides healthful outdoor exercise in addition to good food.

Water Plants

Last weekend's Spoon River Garden Walk was wonderful. All eight gardens were beautiful and inspiring. Every garden included water. In fact, all but one garden had garden ponds. Lockard's did not have a garden pond, but did have fountains and a natural stream.

Obviously, water gardens are extremely popular. They excite our senses. They also allow us to grow a whole group of plants – water plants – that can't be grown otherwise. Many types of water plants are available to accent backyard water gardens, including deep-water plants, bog or marginal plants, oxygenator and submerged plants, and floaters.

Deep-water plants include water lilies and lotus. Perhaps the most spectacular of the deep-water plants is the hardy water lily. They range in color from white to many shades of pink and red. The blossoms are fragrant and last several days, closing every night.

Tropical water lilies offer even more fragrant and vibrant colored blooms. However, they are very susceptible to winter injury and must be removed from the pond and wintered indoors.

Lotus produce very large blooms, that extends as much as 10 inches above the water surface. Their seed pods are attractive and used in flower arrangements. Leaves are a full circle, with the stem coming from underneath like an umbrella. Water lilies, on the other hand, have a split along one side of a circular leaf.

Bog or marginal plants grow at the edge of the pond. Examples include cattails, iris, bamboo, rushes, horsetails, and tall grasses. These plants really make the water garden look like a natural aquatic habitat. They also provide protection for frogs and other pond visitors.

Plants are necessary in water gardens to complete the ecosystem and provide balance. Oxygenator and submerged plants help replenish the water's oxygen supply, absorb carbon dioxide, nutrients, and provide food for fish. Examples include elodea, fanwort, hornwort, and parrot's feather. They are quite winter hardy.

Floating plants help provide cover on the pond's surface, shading the pond and helping prevent algae growth. They simply float in the water and absorb nutrients from the water itself. Examples are fairy moss, water hyacinth, frogbit, water lettuce, and duckweed.

With the proper balance, water gardens require minimal care. Fish help maintain that balance while adding another dimension of beauty. Add fish and plants to your water garden today and enjoy watching an entire aquatic ecosystem in your backyard.

Gardening in Summer

Baldcypress Trees

Last weekend was our 13th annual Kinsel reunion at Anderson Lake. My mother is the youngest of the nine Kinsel children and the reunion gets bigger each year. The week leading up to the reunion includes camping and fishing at Anderson Lake. While there, I noticed several native trees of interest – particularly the baldcypress and cottonwood.

The Common Baldcypress (*Taxodium distichum*) is a large, beautiful tree that is adaptable to a variety of soil conditions. I've seen it growing in many different situations from the dry sands of Mason County to the swamps of Southern Illinois.

In particular, it grows well in and near water so is an obvious choice for the frequently flooding Anderson Lake banks. In fact, the swamps of Southern Illinois have large baldcypress with large "cypress knees." Knees are trunk-like projections that grow out of the water and only occur near water. At one time, people thought they helped the plant's roots obtain oxygen in flooded situations, but research has shown that the "knees" are not necessary for gaseous exchange.

Baldcypress are deciduous conifers. This means they have needle-like leaves that fall off each fall. The rich green foliage is featherlike and turns rusty orange to brown in the fall. It grows 50 to 70 feet tall and 20 to 30 feet wide.

There are also baldcypress at Lakeland Park in Canton.

During my college days, I worked summers for the Canton Park District and helped plant many of the trees at Lakeland Park. The baldcypress there are starting to gain some size and make nice specimen trees.

The other tree we noticed last week was the cottonwood, because "cotton" flew with any slight breeze. The Eastern Cottonwood (*Populus deltoides*) is a common sight among waterways. It has an upright-spreading, vase-shaped habit and can reach large sizes. In fact, it can grow 2 to 4 feet per year to a mature size of 75 to 100 feet and half as wide. The dark green leaves turn a nice yellow in fall.

The "cotton" that flies is actually the fruit. Cottonwoods are dioecious, which means they have female and male trees. All male selections or special hybrids are available that do not produce cotton. This is a somewhat messy tree, but very impressive in the river bottoms.

Both of these trees are native to moist waterways, but also tolerate drier conditions. Always put the right plant in the right place.

Butterfly Gardening

Last weekend my son Derek had a butterfly perch on his hand for several minutes. It was really fun to watch. Butterflies are such beautiful creatures and watching them flit from plant to plant brings joy and relaxation. This is why butterfly gardening continues to grow in popularity.

There are two different types of plants you can grow for butterflies: nectar food sources and larval food sources.

Nectar sources attract the adult butterfly. Many different types of flowers will serve as a nectar source. Avoid planting flowers with double or triple petals (zinnias are an exception). Blue, purple, and white are the favored flower colors to attract butterflies with red probably the least favored color.

Providing larval food plants is where butterfly gardening diverts from all other types of gardening. With these plants you are feeding the caterpillars that eventually turn into adult butterflies. It is hard for many people to allow a critter to eat up their garden plants. However, each type of butterfly larvae eats a specific type of plant. Monarch caterpillars, for example, feed only on milkweed plants, while others feed only on certain trees or herbs.

Butterfly gardens should be colorful, sunny, and sheltered from strong winds. Butterflies are sun worshipers and prefer areas in full sun between 10 a.m. and 4 p.m. Provide rocks and logs for the butterflies to bask. In addition to the variety of flower groups, your garden could include other attractants. Puddles will attract male butterflies to drink and some butterflies prefer to sip juices from rotting fruit. Finally, reduce pesticide use. Butterflies are insects and are susceptible to most insecticides.

Plant your own butterfly garden this summer. Then, sit back and enjoy the show. Butterfly gardening is very rewarding.

Cotoneasters

Last Saturday I enjoyed watching a group of robins out of my kitchen window. If you remember, that was a very windy, cold day and those robins really looked out of place – cold and hungry. They were feeding under our bird feeder and also ate several larger berries off a small cotoneaster plant. I'm assuming that they moved on to warmer country after feasting at my house.

Cotoneasters are excellent plants to use to attract birds and other wildlife. Most cotoneasters are low growing shrubs that can be used to climb over rocks and walls. All varieties have showy berries and many cotoneasters have attractive pink or white flowers as well.

One of the most common cotoneasters is the Cranberry Cotoneaster (*Cotoneaster apiculatus*). This low growing plant grows three feet tall and three to six feet wide. It has small dark green shiny leaves. An even shorter version of that is the Creeping Cotoneaster (*C. adpressus*) that grows only 1-½ feet tall.

The Spreading Cotoneaster (*C. divaricatus*) is much more shrub like. It grows six feet tall and eight feet wide. Like other cotoneasters, it has excellent fall color of fluorescent reddish purple that lasts four to six weeks. This plant is tremendously adaptable and often used in a mass or as a hedge. Professionals say this plant makes a superior hedge to the overused privet (*Ligustrum*) hedge.

One of the most unique and beautiful ones is the Rockspray Cotoneaster (*C. horizontalis*). It has flat, fanlike, herringbone branching patterns of tiny, dark green leaves. It grows three feet tall and eight feet wide.

Daisies

The thought of daisies brings visions of delicate, whimsical flowers. When I think of daisies, I picture the Shasta daisy or painted daisy.

Actually, there are many different types of flowers that could go by the name daisy. Any flower from the Composite family could officially be a daisy. Members of this plant family include dandelions, sunflowers, thistles, asters, marigolds, goldenrod, and the like.

With daisies, what appears to be one flower with multiple petals are actually many, many flowers. On a Shasta daisy, for example, each white "petal" is an individual flower, and the yellow center is made out of many small tubular florets. The white rays are adapted to attract pollinating insects and to give them a landing platform, while the yellow florets contain actual flower parts.

The Shasta daisy (*Leucanthemum* x *superbum*) typically grows one to two foot tall and are most effective in large clumps. The leaves are deep green and coarsely toothed along the edges. Flowers are white and can be single or double.

This year I planted the semi-double cultivar called 'Marconi'. It has white flowers that are five inches wide on three foot tall stems. An old fashioned single flower is 'Alaska' with pure white petals and yellow centers on three inch flowers.

Shasta daisy should be hardy here, but it is sometimes short-lived. Keep trying until you find a variety that works well for you. Better yet, get a start from someone who has a reliable clump of Shasta daisy. This plant does best in full sun, but partial shade is good during the heat of the summer. The soil needs to be well-drained, especially in the winter.

Painted daisies (*Chrysanthemum coccineum*) are a reliable early summer daisy. I have some just ready to pop open in my yard. The flower petals are white, red, or pink with yellow centers. Flowers are three inches across and can be single or double. Leaves are green and fern-like. This plant likes cool weather so does best in late spring and early summer. Cut them back after flowering and they'll flower again in the fall, when it turns cooler again.

For something different, try an English daisy (*Bellis perennis*). This tender perennial is marginally hardy here so it is often planted as an annual flower. Flowers are white, pink or red in early spring. This plant makes a cute six inch clump of dark green leaves with flowers held above the leaves.

Daisies are a must for all flower gardens. Not only are they beautiful, but they are the perfect flower to use to play "He loves me, he loves me not."

Drought Tolerant Plants

I am amazed that plants can grow at all in this summer's hot, dry conditions. Still, certain plants seem to thrive in the hot, dry weather. Take some time to note the plants that are doing well in your yard this year. Here are some notes from my yard this year.

Annuals that are doing well in my yard include nicotiana, celosia, sweet potato vine, marigold, and petunia. We water these plants a couple times a week and they seem to be doing fine, considering the conditions. Some of the other annuals in my yard I have given up on, such as impatiens and nasturtium.

Nicotiana is also called Flowering Tobacco. It is easy to grow and especially valuable for hot, humid areas. The bright pink Avalon hybrid was an award winner in 2001. Plants are seven to ten inches tall. Flowers are one to two inches across with five distinctive petals.

Celosia are also heat and drought tolerant. I grow the plume type and even had some reseed from last year.

The Sweet Potato Vine amazes me. They wilt a little during the day, but keep on growing. Mine are growing down a wall and look great. I have two types: Blackie and Margarita. These ornamental plants provide color and interest like no other plant. They are grown for their distinctive foliage and vigorous growth habit. Ornamental Sweet Potato Vines can be used as an annual groundcover or in hanging baskets and pots.

My perennial bed does not get watered very often. The plants doing well there include black-eyed Susan, purple coneflower, yarrow, and sedum. This makes a lot of sense since these are native plants that do well in our dry prairie conditions.

I've also lost some perennials this year. Several hosta that I divided in the spring have succumbed to the dry heat. I also lost the rest of my hydrangeas. Even the bee balm is struggling to survive this year.

I can also see a difference in the shrubs in my yard. Newly transplanted spirea are struggling, while the established ones are fine – with weekly supplemental watering. The burning bush doesn't like the hot, dry weather and so I have had to give them additional water. I also have several lilac that are drying up, but I think they have borers that are attacking the stressed plants.

Hopefully, you have some plants in your yard that look good in this year of extremes. Keep watering your plants, remembering that thorough deep watering is better than daily sprinkles. Don't forget the established trees, especially evergreens that will need water going into the fall to assure that they don't have major winter injury.

Edible Flowers

Do you want to "spice" up your meals? Sometimes I'll add flowers to a dull looking salad to add color. Or, sometimes I just eat flowers right out in the garden.

But one very important thing that you need to remember is that not every flower is edible. In fact, sampling some flowers can make you very, very sick. Make sure you know for sure the identity of the flower before eating it. You also should **NEVER** use pesticides or other chemicals on any part of any plant that produces blossoms you plan to eat.

Here are a few common, edible flowers to try.

SUNFLOWERS--Almost everyone knows what a sunflower looks like. Choose a mammoth or giant variety. You can harvest the seeds after the petals drop, cure them, and then eat them raw or oven-roasted.

JOHNNY JUMP-UPS (*Viola tricolor*)--This tender perennial has tiny, pansy-like flowers in deep purple, mauve, yellow and white. Blossoms have a mild wintergreen flavor and can be used in salads, to decorate cakes, or served with soft cheese. This plant will do well in sun or shade and grows to a height of six to eight inches.

NASTURTIUMS (*Tropaeolum majus*)--This low-growing annual has blossoms that taste like watercress with a slightly sweet flavor. There are several edible varieties to choose from, most of which grow best in full sun or light shade.

BORAGE (*Borago officinalis*)--This annual ornamental plant produces clusters of one-half inch sky-blue flowers, which bees find particularly attractive. Borage blossoms have a light cucumber taste and can be added to salads, fruit cups, or frozen in ice cubes for cold drinks. Plants grow two to three feet tall.

CHIVES (*Allium schoenoprasum*)--This herb has attractive lavender-pink blossoms that make a delicious addition to salads, egg dishes, and potatoes. Both blossoms and the slender dark green leaves (or "stems") have a subtle onion flavor. This perennial plant likes full sun and grows to one foot.

Father's Day – Insect Repellents

Father's Day is tomorrow and a great opportunity to spend time with your Dad. Like most dads, mine (Ron Simmons) is an important influence in my life and helped instill my love of the outdoors. We have spent many days fishing, camping, and enjoying the outdoors.

Unfortunately, being outdoors often includes insects such as biting flies, mosquitoes, gnats, and ticks. Not only are these a nuisance, but sometimes they also carry disease. The first personal defense is non-chemical – screens, netting, long sleeves, and slacks; but as we all know, that does not always work or is too hot in the summer. The second line of defense is to use an insect repellent.

Insect repellents are available in various forms and concentrations. Aerosol and pump-spray products are intended for skin applications as well as for treating clothing. Liquid, cream, lotion, and stick products enable direct skin application. The most common active ingredient used is DEET, which was developed by the U.S. Army in 1946. It is designed for direct application to human skin to repel insects, rather than kill them.

DEET comes in various concentrations from 4 to 100 %. Lower concentrations are meant for minimal exposure to insects, while higher concentrations may be useful in highly infested areas or for difficult to repel insects. Always use the lowest concentration you can. Research has shown that there really are minimal differences in effectiveness above

15%. I also do not recommend using more than 7 percent on very young children.

The other common ingredients in insect repellents are citronella or other plant extracts. These products do repel insects, but the effects last shorter than DEET. Citronella products usually repel insects for 20 minutes to an hour compared to several hours for DEET products. Still, it works well for some people and can be a good product, especially for those sensitive to DEET.

Finally, remember to reduce the number of mosquito breeding sites outdoors by eliminating containers that will hold water such as old tires and tin cans. Keep eave troughs clean of fallen leaves and other debris so that rainwater drains readily. Empty and clean birdbaths, pet watering bowls, and children's wading pools weekly. Backyard lily ponds and other areas that hold water throughout the summer can be stocked with fish from a local bait shop to eliminate mosquito larvae. Most ponds and lakes are not a major source of mosquitoes because resident fish populations eat the larvae.

Keep screens on windows and doors in good repair. Avoid going outdoors at or shortly after dark or into forested and other areas where mosquitoes are numerous. Mosquitoes are attracted to persons who are wearing dark clothing and perspiring.

Gingko

What tree turns yellow in fall and drops smelly fruit? If you've ever had a female ginkgo tree, you definitely know the answer.

We have a ginkgo tree next to our driveway. It is a really beautiful tree, but two year's ago we discovered it was a female tree when it reached the age to produce fruit. My sons call it the "stinkgo" tree and even have set stink bombs with the fruit under my car tires.

Ginkgo (*Ginkgo biloba*) is a very unique and interesting tree. It is one of the oldest trees known to man, growing on Earth for over 150 million years. Once thought to be extinct, Ginkgo was discovered in China in the mid-1700s and is now grown throughout the world.

This is a large shade tree that reaches about 80' tall by 60' wide at a medium growth rate. Its habit is rather irregular. In youth it is upright columnar, sparsely branched, and open. As it matures it changes to a more spreading growth habit.

The leaves on this tree are very unique. They are fan-shaped and medium green in color. Fall color is rather consistently bright yellow, but a freeze can cause the leaves to drop almost overnight whether they are colored or not.

The one drawback this tree has is it's fruit. Female trees produce tan-orange oval fruits in great abundance, covering the ground with fleshy, bad smelling fruits. Fortunately, the odor is not released unless they are crushed. Crushed fruit smells like vomit. This is because the flesh of the Ginkgo fruit is loaded with butyric acid (a constituent of vomit). However, since our tree is next to the driveway, they are often crushed. Last weekend, I used our shop-vac to sweep them up.

To get around this problem, be sure to plant a male tree. If you don't know the sex of the tree, be sure to place it away from public access areas. 'Autumn Gold' is a male cultivar with more dependable golden-yellow fall color and a broadly pyramidal growth habit at maturity. 'Princeton Sentry' is also male and nearly columnar, and slightly wider at the base, making it a nice vertical accent.

You'll find that this tree is known for other qualities. The nuts within the smelly fruit are a prized delicacy in Asia. Ginkgo extracts are available as herbal supplements.

I highly recommend this tree. Unfortunately, I still don't know what we'll do with ours. I am afraid that as it ages and produces more fruit, the shop-vac and I won't be able to keep up. Unfortunately, we'll probably have to remove the tree.

Groundcovers

Is the only blanket of green in your landscape grass? If so, you may be missing an opportunity to save money, work, and resources. You can enhance your landscape with groundcovers that will outperform grass, require fewer inputs and solve landscape problems.

Groundcovers are a large group of plants that range from 1 inch to 4 feet in height. They come in many different types for many different uses. Some are used in refined landscape areas, while others are more suitable for rugged, naturalized sites.

Some of the most common groundcovers include English ivy, common periwinkle, and purple wintercreeper (*Euonymus*). These are all rather viney plants with woody stems. I particularly like the periwinkle (*Vinca minor*) as it has a bright green color and medium-fine texture. It stays close to the ground at six inches high and spreads widely over time. In the spring it has funnel-shaped, lilac-blue flowers with five perfect little petals.

Other groundcovers are evergreen. They are usually rather coarse in texture. The blue rug juniper is a great example of this. It grows only 6 to 8 inches tall, but spreads 6 to 8 feet wide. It is the lowest growing of the junipers. As the name suggests, it has silvery blue foliage.

Some groundcovers can spread beyond their intended borders. These include goutweed (*Aegopodium*), ajuga, mint, crown vetch, ribbon grass, fleeceflower (*Polygonum*), some sedum, and Lily of the Valley. Although all have good features, they can tend to be quite prolific, taking over areas in the garden if not kept in check. Still, for the right location, these make excellent cover and can help with certain landscape problems. For example, crown vetch has been used extensively in stabilizing steep banks.

There are groundcovers for every situation. For the shady

garden, try pachysandra, hosta, pulmonaria, aromatic sumac, wild ginger, bunchberry, and Lily of the Valley.

Groundcovers are not only beautiful; they also out compete weeds in bare soil areas. Try some today.

Heirloom Plants

Do you like to save seed and "bulbs" from this year's flowers for use next year? Reusing seed and plant parts for use next year is very popular with many people. It is often a tradition passed down from generation to generation, thus passing the flowers on just like china.

Some of our most colorful summer blooms come from tender flowering "bulbs" such as gladiolus, canna, tuberous begonia, and dahlia. However, they are tender and thus do require special care since freezing temperatures kill them. While each requires different growing techniques, they all require similar care in handling.

The "bulbs" of these plants are the root structures and in reality may be tubers, rhizomes, corms, or true bulbs. The root structures of these tender plants must be dug up and stored indoors through the winter. In general follow these steps. Cut the plant back 1-4 inches above the ground once it seems to tire. Then before the first hard frost, carefully dig the root structures up and clean off as much soil as possible. Cure these structures in a warm spot with good air circulation for a few days.

Winter storage should be in a dry, dark location kept at about 45°F. Storage options vary depending on whether the root is fleshy and succulent or dry. Fleshy, succulent roots, such as dahlia, begonia, caladium, and alstromeria must not dry out while stored. Keep them in a box or plastic bags, packed with slightly moist sawdust, peat moss, or wood chips. Dry roots such as gladiolus and cannas can be stored dry in paper bags, onion bags, or old nylon stocking hung where there is good air circulation.

Always label the storage containers carefully so you can

plan next years garden. Remember to check your bulbs, tubers, corms, and roots throughout the storage season and make adjustments as necessary.

Seed collection is easier in some ways, yet complicated with today's technology. If you are growing special hybrid forms or colors, it is likely that seedling plants will not preserve those characteristics. Plant breeders produce these plants in a way that ensures all plants produce similar flowers. When seeds are saved from the hybrid plants, there is no predicting what you will get. In addition, some plants need special conditions to produce seed or do not produce seed that is viable.

There are however some plants that do produce good seed that can be replanted. Some will look like the parent plant, while others may appear slightly different. Simply let the seed mature and then collect it. Collecting and reusing seed is often considering an heirloom task, so ask your grandmother which to collect. My grandmother tells me to collect marigold, zinnia, and poppy, for starters. Passing on heirloom plants may be a bit more work than buying them next spring, but the rewards go on and on.

Iris

Iris was the Greek goddess of the rainbow. Legend has it that she was a member of Juno's court, who was so impressed with her purity that he decided to commemorate her forever with a flower that would bear Iris' name and bloom in the rainbow colors of Iris' robes.

Iris has been grown since times of ancient Egypt and remains beautiful yet today. Iris is truly like the rainbow as they are available in every conceivable combination of colors including blue, white, orange, purple, yellow, and brown-red. Depending on the variety, iris will bloom from early spring to summer.

Iris blooms are unique. The distinctive flowers have six petals. Three reflex downward and are called falls and the other three turn upwards and are called standards. The flower makes a nice cut flower for flower arrangements in the home. It has an average cut life. For the longest life, cut the flower as the bud is about to open since they will continue to develop after they have been arranged.

There are several different types of iris: bearded, Japanese, Siberian, and wild flag, to name a few.

Bearded are the most common and have the most color selections available. They are available as dwarf plants only 4 to 8 inches or full plants up to 36 inches.

Japanese irises are actually bog plants, preferring a moist location. These summer-flowering irises grow 24-36 inches tall.

Siberian irises are also summer bog flowers, although they tolerate drier conditions when watered throughout the growing season.

Dividing the plants easily propagates irises. Do this after flowering (until August). The rhizomes are separated into segments with one set of leaves in a fan and several feeding roots. These are set 1 inch deep and cut the leaves back to 6 inches.

Share iris types among your neighbors, family, and friends. Have an iris dividing party complete with lavender colored cookies and tea.

Real iris enthusiasts might check out the iris societies (www.irises.org). The Prairie Iris Society is located in Pekin.

June Weddings

I was a June bride. My Grandma Simmons told me June brides are extra special. I don't know if that is true, but I sure did feel special that day. Certainly, June is a beautiful month for a wedding. Flowers are a part of all weddings and the bridal bouquet is key.

Bridal bouquets are made of many different types of flowers and can be real, silk, or a combination of both. Prices depend on many factors such as flower type and season. Not all flowers are available year round. For example, one of my favorite flowers is the Lily-of-the-Valley. It is not usually available for June weddings, so one of my University of Illinois professors attempted to force some for me. Unfortunately, it did not work properly so I included silk ones in my bouquet.

Choice and often expensive bridal flowers include eucharis lilies, hybrid and phalaenopsis orchids, camellias, rubrum lilies, lily of the valley, freesia, ivy, and stephanotis. Many of these flowers are fragile, but if prepared properly will last very well in bouquets. Lily-of-the-Valley is wired and taped using a #30 gauge wire wrapped in light green floral tape. Wire and tape help florists control the design of the flower, but in a good bouquet these mechanics will not show.

Moderate priced bouquet flowers include roses, hyacinths, fugi mums, ranunculus, gardenias, tuberoses, and stock. Roses are included in most bridal bouquets because it is the flower of love. Inexpensive flowers in a bouquet might include mums, asters, carnations, daisies, and snapdragons. Greenery is important in a bouquet too (it hides mechanics). Greenery used in the florist industry includes leatherleaf, sprengeri fern, ivy, salal, and more.

The shape and length of the bridal bouquet varies as well. The bride may choose a round colonial or add a cascade to that. There are also clusters, crescents, and basquettes. Clutch bouquets show the individual flower stems, while the others have all stems wrapped in tape and ribbon. Ribbons add whimsical beauty and sometimes color.

Flowers can and are used everywhere at a wedding. They are on the altar, candelabras, pews, kneeling benches, cakes, tables, as corsages, and so much more. The flowers normally used include the bride's bouquet, attendants' bouquets, corsages, boutonnieres, and floral decorations in the church plus reception decorations. There is no limit to the places where flowers can be used.

If you are planning a wedding in the future, remember the

flowers. Consult your florist for a consultation. A professional florist will help make your day extra special – with flowers!

Lilacs

The lilacs have been beautiful this year and many continue to bloom profusely. Lilacs have considerable nostalgia attached to them and are often associated with Grandmother or Mom. My Grandma and Grandpa Simmons had huge lilac bushes that Grandma loved to sit under to enjoy the spring lilac aroma.

If you really like lilacs consider planting several different types together to extend the bloom season. Proper selection can create a garden with up to six to eight weeks of near-continuous lilac blooming.

The hyacinth lilac (*Syringa* x *hyacinthiflora*) blooms from early to mid-May just before the common lilac. This lilac is very hardy. They are large shrubs approaching 10 to 12 feet high and wide. Leaves may turn reddish purple in the fall. Unfortunately, this is not very common and probably hard to find.

The common lilac (*Syringa vulgaris*) blooms from mid-May to early to mid-June depending on the cultivar. Probably 95 percent of the lilacs grown are common lilacs. They come in many colors including white, violet, blue, pink, magenta, purple, and even yellow (actually off-white). The two main types of common lilacs are Fiala's and French. Good cultivars are selected for color, size, form, fragrance, habit of growth and disease resistance.

The Meyer Lilacs (*Syringa meyeri*) are small shrubs that only reach four to eight feet high and has small rounded leaves. Flowers are typically violet-purple and occur in May for about 10 to 14 days. They are spectacular though as they cover the entire plant.

The Miss Kim Lilac (*Syringa patula* 'Miss Kim') is also a smaller lilac that grows four to six feet tall, but the leaves are larger and more pointed. This plant has lilac-purple flowers from May into June.

The Tree Lilac (*Syringa reticulata*) offers a completely different form. This is a small tree that grows 20 to 30 feet high and 15 to 25 feet wide. It flowers from early to mid-June with typically white to off-white flowers. A popular cultivar is 'Ivory Silk' that has heavy flowering and deep green leaves, even at a young age.

Finally, the Late Lilac (*Syringa villosa*) will extend flowering well into summer. Late Lilac blooms from late May into June. However, it's rosy lilac to white flowers are not fragrant, which is a disadvantage to many. This shrub grows six to 10 foot tall, although mine is considerably shorter than the common lilacs next to it.

Mulch

I've received a lot of questions this year concerning mulch. The following information is from Extension Specialists at the University of Illinois and The Ohio State University. I hope it helps clear up any confusion over how mulch affects plants, termites, and fungi.

We recommend mulches around your plants for many reasons. It helps hold moisture, moderate soil temperature, and reduce weeds. We generally suggest use of organic mulch such as compost, leaves, bark, various hulls or shells, and pine needles. Inorganic mulches are materials that do not decompose so they do not add organic matter to the soil. They include such materials as stones and brick chips. Inorganic mulches often serve a purpose in design but are usually more expensive and do not improve the soil.

Unfortunately, moisture in the soil may attract termites to the area and termites may actually eat some mulch. This doesn't mean you should not use mulch around your gardens. However, regardless of which type of mulch you use, never spread it so that it touches the foundation or lowest course of siding on your home.

Flowerbeds and other gardening should never touch the foundation. Never dig up the soil within 12 inches of the house. Digging up the soil or putting new topsoil on top of this area could allow termites access to your foundation.

When planting shrubs, think ahead to how large the plants will be in 10-15 (or more) years. Do not plant shrubs too close to the foundation. Shrubs that are too close to the house may hide termite activity. When necessary, prune shrubs to prevent them from blocking airflow through foundation vents.

In addition to keeping mulch away from the house foundation, you must also keep the mulch at least 4 inches away from the tree trunk. Physical contact of the mulch with the tree is not lethal. Problems occur when the mulch is several inches thick against the trunk. This collar area of the tree needs air exchange. Moisture held up against the trunk does not allow this to happen, and tree decline results.

The other common question we get concerns mushrooms or fungi growing in mulch. These fungi are not harmful to plants. They are growing in the mulch because it is an organic source of nutrients. The fungi also must have moisture to grow. Please don't stop using mulch, don't apply fungicides, and don't stop watering. Instead, rake the bark mulch to dry it out and this will keep mushrooms under control.

Please continue to use mulches around your plants. Follow the above tips to reduce any problems. You'll reap only benefits from your mulch.

Native Plants

Landscaping with native plants has been a trend in the past few years. Certainly, many native plants seemed to survive this summer's drought better than exotics that have been brought here from elsewhere.

Using native plants certainly has advantages. Many examples exist of exotic species taking over native species.

Those that come to mind are kudzu in the south, multiflora rose and purple loosestrife here, and now the dreaded garlic mustard. Each of these was introduced for a reason. If instead a well-chosen native hardwood, shrub, or prairie grass had been used, the same purpose could have been achieved without the problems.

Plantings on the University of Illinois quadrangle are a great example of diversity versus monoculture. The quad was originally planted entirely of American Elms. It was beautiful, but devastating when they all died from Dutch Elm Disease. Next the quad was planted with all thornless honeylocust. Again it was beautiful, but devastating when they all died from a root disease. Today the quad is planted in a variety of plant species, for obvious reasons.

One approach to landscaping your yard with native plants is to think about plant size. Start with dominant or the largest plants first. Look at the woods around us. Large trees form the structure of the woods. Most yards can support at least one white oak, burr oak, or sugar maple.

Next plant the small flowering trees. Several small trees can be used to strengthen the structural diversity of the yard's plantings. These include redbud, flowering dogwood, and ironwood. Sometimes you can bend the "go with natives" principle a bit by using evergreens because they enhance large yards, but don't overdo it.

Finally, add the shrubs, wildflowers, and prairie plants. These form the habitats of your yard such as sunny prairie, woodland wildflowers, native shrub bed, or wildlife area. And don't forget water. Water gardens are very popular and help attract wildlife to your garden.

Ornamental Grasses

Ornamental grasses continue to grow in popularity. There are many different types of ornamental grasses each with it's own beautiful features. However, there are also some grasses that have negative features to consider.

The most popular grasses are bunch type grasses that do best in the heat of summer. Examples include Northern Sea Oats (*Chasmanthium*), Japanese Silver Grass (*Miscanthus* sp.), Hardy Pampas Grass (*Erianthus*), Perennial Fountain Grass (*Pennisetum*), Switch Grass (*Panicum*) and Prairie Cord Grass (*Spartina*). Bunch type grasses form very nice, neat mounds or clumps. They tend to mix very well with other perennials and will not become invasive. They will increase in girth slowly over time.

On the other hand, rhizome forming grasses spread by underground stems and can become very aggressive and invasive. These grasses have their place but it may not be in a well-tended perennial border since they can soon take over an entire area. Before selecting a grass, be sure to understand how it grows so you won't be planting a future problem. Some attractive but aggressive grasses include Blue Lymegrass, Cordgrass, and Ribbongrass.

If you have never tried ornamental grasses or just want to learn more, here are some ways to learn more.

- View ornamental grasses on garden walks in your area.

- Learn about ornamental grasses from home at this University of Illinois Extension website - http://www. urbanext.uiuc.edu/grasses/index.html. It includes sections on understanding ornamental grasses, how to plant, care and maintenance, and types of ornamental grasses.

- Obtain one of the many ornamental grass books at a local bookstore.

- Join a garden club and learn from other members.

Ornamental grasses are beautiful year round and worthy of a spot in your garden.

Poison Ivy - Leaflets Three, Let It Be

My family has been geocaching this summer. This is a high tech treasure hunt and is really fun. We find the coordinates of the treasure on the internet and enter them into our GPS unit. The GPS then guides us to the "treasure." It is an exchange type of treasure hunt, meaning that we take one item and return one item (usually a small trinket such as a matchbox car or yo-yo). Each cache also contains a log to sign and it is fun to see how many others have found that cache. Unfortunately, many caches are hidden in natural areas that contain poison ivy.

Remember the old adage, Leaflets of Three, Let It Be! Poison ivy grows in various locations. It is in fencerows, under trees, and in ornamental shrub and perennial plantings, probably seeded through bird droppings. When growing among desirable plants, poison ivy is a challenge to control.

A member of the sumac family, poison ivy (*Rhus radicans*) has leaflets in threes. Leaflets are entire or with a few, coarse teeth. Although sometimes bushy and erect, poison ivy typically creeps in and around plants and up trees or structures. It has very small green flowers in the late spring and early summer, which develop into gray or whitish berry-like fruit. The fruit is an important food source for many wildlife.

I have done numerous poisonous plant programs and am surprised how few people can recognize poison ivy. Even more surprising is how many people think that Virginia Creeper is a poisonous vine. In fact, many people think Virginia Creeper is Poison Oak. This is just not true. Poison Oak looks similar to poison ivy with three leaflets, but does not grow this far north. Virginia Creeper (*Parthenocissus quinquefolia*) is often confused with poison ivy, however Virginia creeper has leaflets of five, not three, and is not poisonous.

If you think that you have been in contact with poison ivy, it is important to wash yourself and your clothing right away. Plenty of plain old soap and water is your best bet for removing the sap from both skin and clothing. After you have washed thoroughly, apply rubbing alcohol (or other commercial product) to the affected skin. This may sting a little, but it will neutralize any sap that may remain on your skin.

If a rash does develop, paint it with calamine lotion (or other commercial product) to relieve the itching. And if the rash is severe — or it affects the mouth or other sensitive areas of the body — seek medical attention immediately.

Poison ivy rashes certainly are not fun to endure. Yet, for my family, geocaching is so much fun that it is worth the risk. Get a GPS unit and give it a try, but stay away from the "leaves of three."

Raspberries

Have you been enjoying fresh produce this spring? Our family has enjoyed onions, new potatoes, peas, lettuce, spinach, and fresh herbs from our gardens. We also had a nice crop of strawberries this year and are enjoying the wild raspberries right now.

If you don't produce your own fresh produce, consider visiting the Farmer's Market held each Saturday morning at the J.C. Penney parking lot in Canton. This Farmer's Market is sponsored by University of Illinois Extension - Fulton County and always has a wide variety of locally-grown produce available. The market runs from 7:00 a.m. until mid-morning when the produce is gone. July 1st is the first Farmer's Market this year.

Pick up some raspberries for your July 4th desserts. Raspberries ripen shortly after strawberries and thus are in peak production right now. You might also consider growing raspberries at home. There are several different types of raspberries available including red, black, purple, and yellow fruit types.

Red and yellow raspberries have single- and double-cropping types. The double-cropping or everbearing cultivars bear one crop in the early summer and another crop in the fall. A popular red raspberry cultivar for this area is 'Heritage'. It is a widely adapted raspberry with erect canes. 'Heritage' is very dependable and produces firm berries with good flavor. Other red raspberries for central Illinois include 'Ruby' and 'Latham.'

The 'Goldie' yellow raspberry is reported to be a mutation of 'Heritage' so is very similar to it. 'Goldie' is reported to produce medium-large size, round berries, which are deep gold to orange when ripe. Another yellow raspberry is 'FallGold.'

Purple raspberries are not only a beautiful color, but tasty as well. The most popular purple raspberry is 'Royalty'. This is a patented variety and reported to be the best-flavored purple. It can be picked when red to resemble the flavor of a red raspberry or left to darken and develop a flavor more like a black raspberry. Another purple raspberry is 'Brandywine.'

Large black raspberries resemble blackberries, but they are quite different. The difference between a raspberry and blackberry is very simple. When picked, a raspberry leaves its core on the stem and is hollow, whereas a blackberry is solid. The largest black raspberry cultivar is 'Jewel.' This reliable plant produces clusters of large, firm, juicy berries that are great in pies and preserves. Wild berries are typically a black raspberry and not blackberries, although it is possible to find wild blackberries.

For more information on producing your own small fruits (strawberries, brambles, blueberries, currants, gooseberries, and grapes), consider purchasing "Small Fruits in the Home Garden." This book includes information on how to select cultivars, grow the plants to maturity, harvest and store fruits until ready for use, and how to prepare them for family dining. Spiral bound and easy to read, this 78-page book costs just $5.00. It is available at our Lewistown office location. Call 309-547-3711 for more information.

Shade Gardens

Many people consider getting plants established in shady areas of the yard as a challenge. Fortunately, this does not have to be true. There are many options available to gardeners for shady areas. Want to learn more?

What kinds of plants are grown in the shade? The most common ones are hosta and ferns, but there are so many more. Other good herbaceous perennial shade plants include *Heuchera* and *Tiarella*.

Heuchera is known by the common name coral bells. This plant has many attributes and has even been a plant of the year. This plant is pretty at all stages. The leaves form a low non-spreading mound. Red or white flowers are small, bell-like clusters that appear in late spring and summer and are a favorite of hummingbirds.

'Palace Purple' coral bells were the 1991 Perennial Plant of the Year. Purple tinged leaves give the plant its name. The mahogany-red foliage fades to bronze-green during summer heat. The flowers of this variety are white and reach a height of 12 to 24 inches.

New varieties for this year include 'Crimson Curls' and 'Crown Jewel.' 'Crimson Curls' as the name suggests has distinctly curly, crimson foliage with intense crimson color in spring.

The attractive white flowers appear on burgundy stems. In flower the plant is 15 inches across and 18 inches tall. This is a great plant for along borders, as accents, in containers, or in mass. Plant Haven Inc. in Plymouth, Minnesota developed this variety.

'Crown Jewel' was introduced by Clifforrd's Perennial & Vine in Paw Paw, Michigan. This is a dwarf sport of 'Can Can' and only grows 7 inches tall and 9 inches wide. Its ornamental features include heavily ruffled, silver leaves with pewter-gray veins. Its dwarf character makes it a great container plant.

Tiarella is known by the common name foamflower. This plant has lobed, heart-shaped leaves that form a mound. Unlike coral bells, foamflowers do spread to fill in an area. This makes for nice masses of plants in the shady setting, but it is not strong enough to take over entire areas. Flowers are delicate and white reaching a height of 12 to 14 inches.

Be sure to put a bench in your shade garden. You'll want to rest in the shade this summer to enjoy your beautiful plants.

Summer Flowering Bulbs

Summer flowering bulbs are easy to grow and quite beautiful. Among the more popular summer flowering bulbs are tuberous rooted begonia, canna, dahlia, gladiolus, lily, and caladium. Similar plants grown from corms and tubers include daylily, iris, and peony.

Although bulbs, corms, and tubers are all referred to as bulbs, they differ in appearance. A true bulb is composed of layers of flesh, or scales that overlap each other like the layers of an onion. Each year, the growing plant replaces the bulb either partially or entirely. A corm is a swollen underground stem that grows upright. Each year the growing plant produces a new corm on top of the old one. A tuber is the swollen end of an underground side shoot that has an eye, which produces a separate plant.

Summer flowering bulbs are available at most garden supply stores. Most people have some of the plants mentioned here, so consider an exchange with your friends and neighbors. Select healthy, mature bulbs. Make sure bulbs are not diseased. Diseased bulbs look moldy, discolored or soft and rotted. They should be firm and have an unblemished skin. Select varieties that flower together and grow to about the same height. Be sure to get enough of each color and type for a good display in your garden.

Most of these plants need full sun, so select a site that

will provide at least 6 to 10 hours of direct sunlight a day. Prepare the soil in the planting site thoroughly. Plant at depths, distances apart, and planting times recommended for each kind of bulb. Water the planted beds thoroughly to help settle the bulbs into the soil.

Some of the summer flowering bulbs are not hardy here and therefore must be dug up in the fall and stored for planting the following year. These include begonia, caladium, dahlia, canna, and sometimes gladiolus.

One of the most commonly grown summer flowering bulbs is the peony. Peony grows 2 to 4 feet tall. It blooms in late spring and early summer. Various flower colors are available depending upon the cultivars selected. Flowers are 3 to 6 inches across and very fragrant. Flower types include single, double, and anemone. Divide these plants in late summer into sections containing 3 to 5 eyes. Set divisions about 1 inch below the soil surface. Deeper planting delays or inhibits flowering.

There are literally thousands of daylily cultivars from which the daylily fancier can choose. Daylilies are so named because individual flowers are short-lived. They vary in height from 6 inches to 6 feet and come in many flower colors. Tubers should be planted just below the surface of the soil in early spring or late summer. Divide plants every 3 or 4 years and share with a friend.

Sunflowers

Sunflowers are popular. It seems one can find a sunflower on almost anything, from throw pillows to towels to floor mats and rugs. I've also noticed more and more gardeners growing sunflowers. My cousins (Lyle and Kyle Harris) have large sunflowers growing at the corners of their vegetable garden. Home gardeners grow sunflowers for their beauty, for their tasty seeds, or for wild bird feed.

Some varieties grow extremely tall, while others have been developed for ornamental use with multiple yellow, red, white or a combination of colored flower heads. My husband and I planted long annual hedges this year using sunflowers. We used a tall one in the back and a shorter sunflower mix in the front. As they get taller they will screen our wiener-roast area.

Sunflowers (*Helianthus annuus*) are easy to grow and even tolerate heat and drought. Simply sow the seeds, after danger of frost, in the sunny garden. For best results, thin plants 2 to 4 feet apart, depending on ultimate size.

In recent years, breeders have developed more short sunflowers for the garden. 'Teddy Bear' is a nice short one (24") with a showy, fuzzy, fluffy flower. This double flower is brilliant golden yellow with no "centers". 'Sunspot' looks more like the traditional sunflower, but only grows 2 ½ feet tall.

'Mammoth Russian' and 'Grey Striped' are tall varieties at 6-12 feet tall that bear large 12 to 24 inch seed heads. 'Giant Sungold' is a full-sized version of the dwarf Teddy Bear. It grows 10-inch, super-double flowers on 6 to 7 foot plants.

One of the 2000 All America Selection winners this year is a dwarf Mexican sunflower (*Tithonia rotundifolia*). 'Fiesta Del Sol' thrives on summer heat and humidity attaining a mature height of 2-3 feet. The single, orange daisy flowers are 2-3 inches across. Like true sunflowers, Mexican sunflowers make excellent cut flowers and may attract butterflies.

If you feed birdseed to the birds, you may find a few volunteer sunflower plants popping up here and there. When the plants are small they can be transplanted to another part of the garden if necessary. Incidentally care must be taken when feeding sunflower seeds because an accumulation of hulls under the feeder kills grass and other herbaceous vegetation. In fact, very few plants besides sunflowers will grow in these areas due to a chemical in the sunflower hulls. Remove the hulls regularly or site the feeder where there is no danger of damage to lawns or other desirable vegetation.

Sunflowers can be planted almost anywhere. Add some cheer to your garden with sunflowers.

Tomato Woes

I've had many calls this year concerning the most popular homegrown vegetable - tomatoes. Although typically very easy to grow, tomatoes are prone to some problems. This year's cool, wet conditions have results in increased tomato disease.

Many tomato growers are experiencing leaf diseases this year such as septoria leaf spot and early blight. These produce small spots on the lower leaves. In wet weather conditions, they can defoliate plants from the bottom up. When leaves are lost, the tomato fruit is exposed to sunscald (whitish areas on the fruit). To manage these diseases keep all ripe fruit picked off plants, improve air circulation in the garden, mulch to avoid fruit rots, and remove tomatoes and vines at the end of the season. University of Illinois specialists also suggest using a two- to three-year crop rotation to reduce losses from these diseases.

There are fungicides labeled for use on tomatoes to control tomato leaf diseases, such as maneb. They are sold under many different trade names, so read the label carefully to be sure you purchase the right product. Look for a product that lists tomatoes and says it controls the diseases I've mentioned. Read and follow all directions carefully. These fungicides often need repeated applications at certain intervals to work properly. Most importantly, follow any harvest intervals to be sure the produce is safe when you eat it.

Later blossom-end rot may become a problem for some growers. Blossom-end rot appears as brown or black areas at the blossom-end of the maturing fruit. Tomato, pepper, summer squash, and other cucurbit crops may show this problem. This is not a disease, but rather results from low calcium levels in the plant. This usually occurs during dry periods when the plant grows slower and takes up fewer nutrients from the soil. The best way to manage this is to maintain even and adequate soil moisture. Applying calcium-rich fertilizer to the foliage has mixed reviews. Some studies indicate that some control is achieved, while others report little or no reduction in the condition.

Vines

I enjoyed talking to many of you last Saturday at the Canton and Farmington Garden Walks. The response to the walks was overwhelming. Thank you to the garden owners for sharing their beautiful gardens with us. I know you all worked hard to prepare and the results were just spectacular.

All the gardens had something to offer and I learned something at each location. What really struck me, though, were the number of vines and their uses. When used properly, vines really catch the eye by adding a new dimension to the garden.

In Canton, I was at the Meade residence most of the day. The most common question of the day was "What is that growing on the fence?" The vine they were referring to is Porcelain Vine (*Ampelopsis brevipedunculata*). Kevin and Terry Meade have the variegated one called 'Elegans'. Porcelain vine is named for its handsome fruit that is probably unrivaled by any other woody plant in vitality of color. The ¼" diameter berry changes from yellow to pale lilac and finally to bright blue; often with all colors present in the same cluster. 'Elegans' leaves are variegated white, green, and pinkish. This cultivar is especially nice because it is not as vigorous as the species.

Also at the Meade residence was the unique and somewhat rare Arctic Beauty Kiwi (*Actinidia kolomikta*). This particular Actinidia has uniquely decorated leaves. They are pink at the tip, white in the middle, and green at the base. The White Flower Farm catalog indicates that they "offer male plants only, because they have the best coloring and note that leaf color takes a year or two to develop."

Several locations displayed the Mandevilla (*Mandevilla*

x *amabilis*) vine. This woody twiner has large showy pink flowers and blooms in profusion over long periods. The dark green, glossy leaves are also attractive.

Other vines displayed included clematis, wisteria, honeysuckle, trumpet vine, and many different groundcovers. The Martin residence in Farmington had both clematis and wisteria. Clematis is available in many flower colors from white to pink to dark wine-red to lavender to deep purple. The selection is almost endless. This vigorous growing vine grows well on walls, trellises, fences, or any supporting structure.

Wisteria flowers are outstanding and often fragrant. Wisteria is easy to grow, but sometimes difficult to get to bloom. The reasons vary including too much nitrogen, winter injury, and the need for pruning. Too much nitrogen promotes excess vegetative growth and few flowers. Sometimes it helps to cut vigorous growth back to 3 or 4 buds since some species bloom on the current season's growth. It is also usually advisable to use named cultivars rather than seedling-grown material.

Vegetable Gardens

Last Saturday I judged vegetables at the 4-H General Show in Lewistown. Congratulations to all who exhibited as the vegetables were excellent. We certainly have a great bunch of future gardeners.

Most vegetable gardens are certainly producing well right now. I have enjoyed many fresh vegetables from my own garden including broccoli, zucchini, cucumbers, corn, onions, and potatoes.

Most vegetable gardens provide ample produce for the family and often for friends and neighbors as well. Proper preservation of the produce is necessary to assure it is available for later use. There are four basic ways to preserve foods – storage, drying, canning, and freezing. Each vegetable varies in its adaptability to different preservation methods.

To assure food is safe, University of Illinois Extension

— Fulton County offers pressure cooker checks for cookers/ canners with mechanical gauges. The check is done right in our office and checks to be sure that the pressure gauge accurately measures the pressure inside the cooker. Please call ahead to arrange for the check.

If you have harvested part of your garden, now is the time to begin your fall garden. A fall garden extends your supply of fresh vegetables. Unfortunately, a successful fall garden demands additional work and planning at a time when you are busiest. Irrigation is usually necessary and weeds grow quickly at this time. But the pleasure you can derive from a fall garden far outweighs the extra effort involved in planning and planting it.

The midsummer planting usually takes place from July 10-20 and could include snap beans, beets, broccoli plants, cabbage plants, carrot, cauliflower plants, and okra. From August 1-10 you could also add many cool-crops such as lettuce, mustard greens, turnips, and winter radishes. Spring radishes, spinach, and more leaf lettuce can go in as late as August 25 to September 5.

If you don't have a vegetable garden, consider visiting a local Farmers Market.

Water Landscape Plants

Where is the rain! This year is quickly becoming one of the driest in history. If your yard is like mine, your landscape plants are suffering from the dry conditions. The rapid onset of poor looking landscape plants is cause for concern.

As a rule of thumb, landscape plants need about an inch of water a week. The easiest way to attain this is with a sprinkler or soaker hose. Set out a can or cup and quit watering when you've collected an inch of water.

Here are some tips that might help with your watering. Clay soils tend to stay wet longer, but are harder to rewet once they turn to glazed pottery. Anything planted this year and any trees or shrubs planted over the last two years need extra water. New plantings and containers may need to be watered daily. Vegetables and fruit plantings need water especially when they are forming fruit. Even plants listed as drought tolerant will need extra water if just planted.

Please don't ignore your old trees and shrubs because mature woody landscape plants often do not exhibit symptoms from underwatering for several months. Younger plants show symptoms much sooner. When symptoms are evident they could include severe leaf wilt, yellow leaves, early fall coloring, and leaf scorch (browning along the margins).

Symptoms are a result of the roots failing to supply enough water to the leaves. This inability is influenced by the moisture content of the soil and by the location and condition of the root system. The drought conditions have significantly reduced some plant root systems, making them unable to supply enough water to compensate for the tremendous amounts lost through the leaves.

As would be expected, some plants are affected more by drought conditions than others. Especially affected are potentilla, hydrangea, viburnum, euonymus, and holly shrubs; redbud and maple trees; spruce, pine, and hemlock conifers; and bog plants such as iris and astilbe. Fortunately, our native prairie species adapt well to these conditions and although the top growth may suffer, the dieback helps build reserves into the crown for growth next season.

Save your landscape plants! Water stressed plants to encourage recovery growth and root revival. Watch our weather patterns and water during this drought period. Water slowly and deeply. Watering thoroughly once a week is much better than watering a little every evening. Light, frequent watering can lead to shallow rooting and increased disease, weed development, and insect damage. Never overwater your plants.

Gardening in Fall

Asters and Mum

Fall provides us with brilliant colors: orange pumpkins, yellow mums, purple asters, and bronze autumn joy sedums. The fall flower garden has a lot to offer and brings a change in flower color.

Most people think of mums as the main fall flowering plant. Mums are important, but don't rule out asters, sedums, Japanese anemone, and ornamental grasses.

Asters bloom in later summer into early fall. Asters have colorful, yellow-centered daisy flowers of blue, purple, white, pink, and red. Heights range from 6 inches to 6 feet depending on the type grown.

For a nice fall planting, try some of the asters like *Aster* x *frickartii* 'Monch.' This is a sturdy plant that remains under 3 feet tall. It has lavender blossoms above dark green, mildew-resistant leaves. Many of the native asters such as the New England Aster (*Aster novae-angliae*) can reach up to 5-6 feet and require staking. They make nice cut flowers for fall flower arranging.

Fall mums are an old time staple of the fall garden. There are types available that offer early, mid-season, and late color. Heights vary from one to five feet tall. In order to keep them compact, pinch them during the summer.

Garden mums come in all colors except blue and in many forms from daisy to pompon, to button to full cushion. If you want the mum to come back each year in the garden, be sure to purchase a hardy mum. It is not too late to plant your garden mums. Soil temperatures are warm enough to allow ample root growth and establish the plants for the winter. Remember to pinch (cut) them back a couple of times during the summer.

There are also many beautiful berries at this time of year. Examples include hollies, hawthorn, chokeberries, and crabapples. While walking to the University of Illinois football game last weekend, I noticed an awesome display of red chokeberry (*Aronia Arbutifolia*). The fruit is bright red, firm and glossy and last well into January.

Take time this fall to notice the beauty around you. Trees show their colors, fall perennials are at their peak, fall fruit displays are evident, and fall decorations abound. Best of all, temperatures are great for a fall walk to enjoy it all!

Bagworms

Bagworms have hatched throughout Illinois! June is the best time to control them, so act fast! If you have seen bagworms on any of your plants in the past, check them in June for activity.

There are several different insects that people call bagworms, including the tent caterpillars and webworms. The bagworm I am referring to is smaller and builds individual diamond shaped bags all over the plants.

Bagworms attack a wide range of evergreen and deciduous trees and shrubs (128 plant species), including arborvitae, juniper, eastern red cedar, spruce, fir, pine, maple, box elder, crab-apple, hackberry, and black locust.

Small grayish, black colored worms emerge from last year's bags in early June in central Illinois. They are so small that you will not notice them without careful inspection, but they have begun to feed upon whatever leaf material is present. Unfortunately, they are usually not noticed until significant damage is done. Because young larvae migrate to the tops of trees and shrubs, look in these areas for early infestations.

Do not wait to treat. You can manually pick the small bags off and kill them, but they are hard to find at early stages. Fortunately, the small caterpillars are very susceptible to insecticide treatment when small. In central Illinois, the larvae will have finished their ballooning by July so a single application of *Bacillus thuringiensis kurstaki* (Dipel, Thuricide), cyfluthrin (Tempo), or other pyrethroid should provide control for the season.

I recommend using the biological insecticide *B.t. kurstaki* (Dipel, Thuricide) as it affects only caterpillars of moths and caterpillars. Do not wait, as the insecticide is not effective once the bags are larger and the caterpillar has pupated. As always, be careful when using any pesticide and read label directions carefully.

In a few weeks the caterpillar changes from a larval (caterpillar) stage to a resting (pupa) stage. Later in the year they will emerge from the pupa within the bag as either wingless, nearly legless females or furry, black, winged males. The females remain in the bag, but the males leave it behind in search of females to mate with. Females lay nearly 500 eggs per bag and then die. The bag serves as over wintering protection for the eggs that will hatch next June in central Illinois.

Bring Houseplants in Now

Did you get your houseplants moved indoors in time? I was one of those who scrambled around to move plants in at the last possible moment. Now the houseplants are indoors it is time to groom and clean them. While you are at it, also consider "fall-cleaning" the plants that remained indoors during the summer.

Clean and groom plants to keep them healthy, clean, and attractive. Also, check each plant to see if it has become root-bound. If it is outgrowing its pot, repot it into a bigger pot using a good potting soil mix.

Clean plant leaves to remove dust and dirt build-up

with 1-teaspoon non-phosphate soap in 1 quart of water. Commonly used soaps include Ivory dish soap and PineSol, but many others are okay too. Use a sponge, cleaning cloth, or paper towel to wipe all surfaces of the leaves clean. Wipe down containers too.

Another cleaning option is to spray plants with a non-ammonia glass-cleaning product (such as Sparkle) and wipe clean. Hairy plants should be cleaned only with a brush or feather duster.

Groom plants by removing debris. Debris found on the plant, on the top of the soil, or at the bottom of the container should be cleaned out regularly. Keep the plant attractive by trimming off old flower heads and all dead or dying leaves. Plants kept outdoors during the summer may need pruning to fit back indoors. Isolate the plants from those already in the house until they are determined to be pest-free.

Do not despair if some leaves drop after moving the plant indoors. The plant will need to adjust to differences in light levels and watering. Most growing conditions in a home only allow plants to maintain current growth. Some plants, such as *Ficus*, will adjust to lower light levels by dropping leaves and forming new ones. Others will simply drop lower, older leaves. Water carefully since they will not require as much water as they did outside. The most common mistake homeowners make indoors is watering too much.

Finally, do not fertilize houseplants in the winter. Plants only need fertilizer when they are actively growing. In the winter, most houseplants do not grow much and therefore do not typically need fertilizing.

Moving nature back indoors for the winter allows homes to come alive. In fact, recent studies indicate that houseplants help keep people happier and healthier. Plants fill an important psychological function and are also proven to cleanse indoor air. Enjoy your plants as you move them in. If you don't have a houseplant, go buy one.

Caladiums

This year I planted lots of caladium in my flowerbeds. They are the spotlights of the front of our house and our back entrance. Their colorful, tropical foliage with big wafer-thin leaves always looks great.

Caladium (*Caladium* x *hortulanum*) is known by many different common names including fancy-leaved caladium, elephant's ear and angel-wings. The plants are grown for their showy leaves not their flowers. There are many different cultivars to choose from offering leaf color variations with green, white, pink, and red tones.

Four cultivars are most popular. 'Frieda Hemple' leaves have a dark green edge with a solid red center. 'Fannie Munson' is described as a pink leaf with a narrow, green margin. 'Red Flash' is my favorite. It has large waxy leaves with bright red center, deep red veins, pink mottling and green edging. 'Candidum' has a snow- white leaf with prominent green veins and a green margin.

Caladium's are fast growing and do well in a variety of soil conditions. They grow 1 to 2 feet tall in full sun to partial shade. They look best as a specimen plant, container plant, or massed in a border. I have a massing of caladium's in a flowerbed I call the kid's garden, because it is near the swingset. It contains the large elephant's ear, smallers caladiums, money plant, and lambs-ear around a red Radio-flyer wagon planted with Verbena.

Caladium's are tropical plants and therefore do not overwinter here. With some work, however, we can overwinter the root structures indoors. While digging your caladium's, you should also dig the other tender flowering "bulbs" such as gladiolus, canna, and tuberous begonia. Most summer flowering bulbs should be dug and stored when the leaves on the plants turn yellow. Carefully lift them from the ground and cut the tips an inch above the root structure.

Leave the soil on begonia, canna, caladium, dahlia, and

bulbs. Store these bulbs in clumps on a slightly moistened layer of peat moss or sawdust in a cool place. For all other summer bulbs wash off loose soil that clings to the bulbs. Spread the washed bulbs in a shaded place to dry. When dry store them away from sunlight in a cool, dry place.

If you have only a few bulbs, you can keep them in paper bags hung by strings from the ceiling or wall. For large numbers of bulbs, be sure air can circulate around your bulbs and never store more than two or three layers deep. Be sure to separate your bulbs by species or variety and label them well.

Canna Lily

Last weekend we went to the Illinois State Fair (2003). The flowers on the state fairgrounds are extra beautiful this year. There is lots of color and variety among the flowerbeds. Scattered throughout the grounds are also several tall poles with hanging baskets that rival those at major amusement parks.

Mom and I especially liked the canna lilies there. I've had other people tell me that their canna lilies are exceptional this year. Canna lilies like wet soil, so maybe the timely rains we've received have helped them to thrive better this year. They also prefer full sun with rich, fertile soil.

Cannas are large plants that grow one to five feet tall. The leaves are quite large, growing to two feet long and six inches wide or wider. The foliage may be blue-green, green, purple or variegated.

Canna flowers are four to six inches across. This is a tall, upright plant and the flowers are also strongly upright. Flowers are red, yellow, orange, pink, white, variegated or speckled. Canna actually comes in two flower types: orchid-flowered and gladiolus-flowered. Gladiolus flowers are most popular. The flowers last a long time from mid to late summer.

The canna that caught our eye at the State Fair was the 'Bengal Tiger' Canna. This is indeed a beautiful canna. It has dramatic stalks of green and yellow striped leaves with a brilliant maroon edge that grows to six feet. The plant is topped in summer with bright orange flowers. 'Bengal Tiger', like many other cannas, will also grow in water as an aquatic plant.

Canna lilies are tender perennials, meaning that they are perennials in milder climates but must be replanted each spring here. The rhizome roots are dug after the first frost has killed the tops. Store the rhizomes in moist peat moss at 40-50 degrees F for best results.

Another variety to try is the Tropical Rose Canna. This plant won the All America Selection award in 1992. It grows about 2 ½ feet tall and has a soft, rose-colored flower. Many people like this canna because it is shorter and can be grown from seed. For best results the seed should be started indoors in late winter. The tropical canna is also available now in red and salmon too.

Cannas work well as massed displays and in containers. The best displays I've seen this year were in containers. The State Fair had many large pots in a mixture of plants surrounding a large canna in the center. Tall Timbers Marina in Havana also has gorgeous pots with cannas placed on the docks.

Chestnuts

Chestnuts roasting on an open fire... This is my favorite Christmas song. Yes, I know it is still two months until Christmas, but chestnuts are in peak season now. At my sister's (Lynn Miller) surprise birthday party last weekend, we gathered and roasted chestnuts.

My sister's home grounds include many different nut trees including walnut, chestnut, pecan, and buckeye. Several "squirrels" at the party went out in the dark with flashlights to gather buckeyes and chestnuts.

The real chestnuts (*Castanea* spp.) belong to the Fagaceae family (beech), while the buckeyes belong to the Hippocastanaceae family. The seeds of the buckeye are potentially poisonous and should not be eaten. To distinguish between the edible chestnuts and the buckeye, it is helpful to look at the fruit and leaves.

In *Trees Worth Knowing* by Julia Ellen Rogers, the edible chestnut is aptly described as follows: "The nut of this tree is hung high aloft, wrapped in a silk wrapper, which is enclosed in a case of sole leather, which again is packed in a mass of shock absorbing, vermin proof pulp, sealed up in a waterproof, ironwood case, and finally cased in a vegetable porcupine of spines, almost impregnable. There is no nut so protected; there is no nut in our woods to compare with it as food."

The difference in the husks is that the buckeye has a woodier husk with thick spikes, whereas the edible chestnut is encased in a burr of dense spines resembling a sea urchin. An easy way to tell the difference between the buckeye and the edible chestnut is by the leaf shape. The buckeye has a palmate compound leaf with five to seven leaflets radiating from its center. The buckeye is a common landscape tree known for its showy flowers that bloom in early spring.

There was a time when chestnuts were abundant in our woods. The American Chestnut (*Castanea dentata*), once a magnificent and noble tree of the eastern North American forests, was devastated by a blight. Today trees of Chinese or Korean origin replace them. Those chestnuts available in stores during the fall are usually of European origin.

The most popular method of cooking chestnuts is roasting. DO NOT roast a chestnut until each shell has been punctured or else you will have exploding chestnuts. To peel a fresh chestnut, score the flat side with an "x." Simmer the chestnuts in water, or roast at 350°, until shells begin to curl. Using a paring knife, remove shells and skins while chestnuts are hot.

In addition to eating freshly roasted, chestnuts are used in stuffings, cakes, and many other dishes. Chestnuts are low in fat compared with other nuts and are high in carbohydrate and dietary fiber. Try some!

Chiggers

I've had several calls this year about chiggers. There are many wife's tales and misconceptions about chiggers. Chiggers are microscopic mites. That means that they are very tiny and have eight legs. They are also ectoparasites, which mean that they live on the outside of the host's body.

Chiggers cause a rash known as chigger dermatitis. Chigger dermatitis causes the skin to speckle with rather large, raised, red spots that itch ferociously. Chiggers prefer constricted areas such as sock tops, waistbands or armpits. The spots are caused by the feeding activity of the tiny mites.

Contrary to popular belief, chiggers do not bury beneath the skin or suck blood. Chiggers inject a salivary fluid that dissolves the host's cells, and then they suck up the liquefied tissue. Within a few hours, small, reddish, intensely itching welts appear. These bites may continue to itch for several days up to two weeks after the chigger is dislodged.

As with other insect problems, it seems that some people are more prone to chiggers than others. Similar to mosquitoes, the chigger is attracted to the carbon dioxide that our bodies give off. Chiggers are typically more prevalent in tall grass, weeds, shrubby plants, or berry brambles.

To control chiggers in your yard, University of Illinois recommends eliminating or mowing breeding sites, especially tall grass, weeds, and other thick vegetation where there is an abundance of moisture and shade. You can treat lawns, roadsides, and areas not mowed with Sevin. Remember that Sevin is a pesticide and must be used carefully according to label directions!

You can protect yourself from chiggers in much the same way that you protect yourself from mosquitoes and ticks. Wear protective clothing such as long-sleeved shirts and trousers, shoes and socks. Tuck pant legs into boots or socks. Avoid sitting on the lawn or on the ground in brushy areas. Take a warm, soapy shower or bath immediately after returning from any infested areas to kill or dislodge the chiggers.

Apply a repellent containing DEET to shoes, socks and trousers before entering chigger-infested areas. Always use repellents properly. Do not use on children less than two years of age or use more than 10% DEET on children between the ages of 2 and 12.

When bites begin to itch, one course of treatment is to apply rubbing alcohol, followed by one of the non-prescription local anesthetics. A baking soda paste, calamine lotion, or "After-Bite" product may help reduce discomfort. Avoid scratching bites since this only increases irritation and may lead to secondary infection of the bite.

Cobwebs

While driving to a morning meeting this week, I couldn't help notice the abundance of spider webs shining in the weeds along the road. The dew allowed many to show up perfectly. Spiders are abundant (over 1,000,000 individuals per acre in a grassy field) and can be found almost anywhere from the bedroom closet to the 22,000-foot level on Mt. Everest.

Spiders are a common image this time of year because of Halloween. Webs are often associated with abandoned, neglected, or haunted houses, while the animals themselves bring to mind the image of a painful or deadly bite. Actually, spiders are beneficial, feeding mostly on small insects and other arthropods.

Not all spiders use webs. Some do trap their prey in webs or snares; others are active hunters that use excellent vision to stalk or ambush their food. Virtually all spiders have poison glands that connect with the fangs. Venom produced by the glands is used to kill or paralyze prey. Only a few species, such as the black widow and the brown recluse, have venom that is very toxic or harmful to humans.

There are about 2,500 different species in North America. Some live in holes in the ground while others may be found under rocks or logs. Most spiders found in homes and buildings are "accidental invaders" that have entered around doors, windows, or other openings. Homes in wooded areas or with naturalized or landscaped foundations may be prone to more frequent invasion because the surroundings are ideal spider habitats.

Most spiders in homes and gardens build neat, organized webs or sheets of webbing that lead into a funnel. A spider often found in gardens is the Black and Yellow Argiope. Its web is very interesting because it usually has crossed zigzag bands. The large, conspicuous spider hangs head down in the center of the web.

Household spiders that spin cobwebs are usually found in secluded areas in and around the home. These spiders feed on other spiders and insects, including such household pests as flies and moths. The more insects there are inside the home, the more likely spiders will live there.

To manage household spiders, knock down webs with a broom or duster. Vacuuming works well too. Keep screens and other openings in good repair. Caulk all seams around windows and doors. If you must use a chemical spray, be sure it is labeled for household use to control spiders and follow directions carefully. Do not use outdoor chemicals in your home!

Deer Damage

Deer hunting season is upon us and so it seems appropriate to do an article about deer damage to landscape plants. Fall and winter is a time when deer can cause major damage to landscape plants. Two types of damage can occur; antler rubbing occurs during the fall, while browsing is more of a concern during the winter.

Antler rubbing is done by males during the mating season. They typically select saplings approximately 5 years of age and older, often rubbing the entire circumference of the tree, causing early death of the plant.

Browsing occurs during the winter, and can be especially severe in winter with long lasting snow cover. Damage can be over six feet above ground level. Deer browsing is one of the primary plant damage concerns in both natural and residential areas. Since the average deer eats 6 to 8 pounds of plants per day, this can add up to substantial injury or death to landscape material.

There are several options to lessen the potential for damage to plants.

Deer like woodland edges. One way to lessen the potential for damage is to have as much open area between woodland edges and landscape plants as possible.

Another option is to put in plants deer don't like to eat. These include plants such as boxwood, barberry, and Colorado blue spruce. Other plants that are seldom severely damaged include honey locust, red osier dogwood, and Norway spruce.

Repellents may help in small areas. They will not eliminate damage, but may reduce it. Contact repellents work as a taste deterrent. Area repellents are odor deterrents. Repellents should be applied by mid fall to early winter. Reapplications are usually needed to extend the effectiveness of the product.

There are many types of fencing that effectively protects plants from deer damage. Wire or plastic mesh, electrified fence (vertical or slanted), and polywire options are available, based on deer pressure and the amount of protection desired.

For more information on deer damage control, visit the University of Nebraska Prevention and Control of Wildlife Damage website at http://icwdm.org/handbook/index. asp#om.

Fall Color

The Spoon River Scenic Drive not only offer crafts and history, but also an opportunity to witness beautiful fall color. It is very hard to predict whether or not we will have a great fall color. Hopefully, this will be a good year.

Fall color is controlled by the plant's genetic factors and the weather. There are three possible kinds of color pigments present in plant leaves depending on the species: green (chlorophyll), yellow/orange, and red. During the short days and cool temperatures of autumn, plants produce fewer green pigments. With fewer greens, the leaves start to show their other colors.

You can use fall leaf color to help identify different tree species. As you drive around the county on the Spoon River Drive, look for these leaf colors on the trees. Oaks will be red, brown or russet. Hickories are a golden bronze. Dogwoods turn purple-red, and are at peak color this weekend. Birches will be a bright yellow, while Poplars are golden yellow. Maple trees show a whole range of colors: Sugar Maple is orange-red, Black Maple is glowing yellow, and Red Maple is bright scarlet.

Trees also color at different times. Fall color starts in September with the brilliant reds of poison ivy and sumac and ends in November with the dull yellow larches and weeping willows. Frost and freezing temperatures will stop the coloration process and blacken the leaves.

What factors produce great fall color? Well, it is actually very scientific, but weather is a big factor. Typically, a warm, cloudy fall with much rain will result in less fall color show. Warm, sunny days and cool nights help increase the color intensity. This must happen gradually. As the leaves stop producing chlorophyll, the other colors build up inside. A warm, sunny day causes more intense colors as the cool, long nights help shut down chlorophyll production.

Enjoy the beauty this fall. Go on the Spoon River Drive.

Go for a walk in the park. Fall color happens only once a year, so take advantage of this opportunity. You can even take the experience one step further with a fall foliage activity. Collect different colored leaves and make a fall bouquet, wreath, or mosaic. For more ideas, go to our University of Illinois Extension website about fall fun at http://www. urbanext.uiuc.edu/fallcolor/fun.html

Fall Garden Activities

This week I worked on cleaning up my gardens for winter. Hopefully, fall garden activities done now will reduce the amount of spring cleanup next year. Fall is a great time to be outdoors and there are many gardening activities that need attended to.

Garden cleanup is the most obvious activity. Now is the time to clear away leaves, dead stems, and trash. Put this debris in your compost pile where it will turn into valuable organic matter that can later be returned to the soil.

After cleanup is complete, the next step is fertilization. Fall is a perfect time to fertilize and water your woody landscape plant material. The cooler air temperatures and shorter day length signal the plants to move into their winter dormancy period.

The recommended time of late fall fertilizing is after the first hard October freeze through December. Don't worry about the extra fertilizer causing the plant to break dormancy. This happens only after the plant has been exposed to a certain amount of cold temperatures. Plants leaf out in the spring after their cold requirements have been met. It is important however to fertilize after the leaves have fallen. Fertilizing earlier can cause problems.

Evergreens (needle and broad leaf types) also enter a period of winter rest but their foliage doesn't drop. Evergreens also benefit from a late fall, early winter-feeding as well as deep fall watering. Since evergreens keep their foliage all winter, winter winds can dry out the needles, removing any excess moisture that might be stored. Provide ample fall moisture to avoid this. You can also apply an anti-desiccant spray, which reduces the moisture loss from the needles and broad leaves. These are available at most garden centers. Read and follow all label directions, paying special attention to any second applications recommended in January or February.

Finally, winter mulch should not be applied until the ground begins to freeze, usually late November. Applying winter mulch too early can delay the natural hardening process and attract rodents. Remember, the purpose of most winter mulches is to keep the plants cold, not warm.

Other activities you can do now include wrapping young and newly planted trees that are susceptible to frost cracks or rodent feeding. Dig and store tender bulbs and corms such as gladioulus, dahlia, canna, and caladium. Collect soil samples, if needed. Finally, make sure to clean and repair garden tools before storing them away for the winter. Enjoy your fall in the garden!

Fall Lawn Care

Early fall is the ideal time to think about lawn care activities. Most Illinois lawns are made up of cool season grasses that thrive in late fall, early winter, and spring. Summer's temperatures put more stress on the plants than any other time of the year.

A few hours spent on the lawn this fall will be paid back next year. Aerating and fertilizing can increase the vigor of the root system and shoots. Dethatching may be necessary if too much thatch is present. Fall is also an ideal time to consider broadleaf weed control.

If you only fertilize your lawn once a year, this is the time to do it. Early fall (August 15 – September 15) is a key time for fertilizing lawns in central Illinois. An easy way to remember it is by using holidays. If you fertilize once a year, do it at Labor Day; two times a year, Labor Day and

Mother's Day; three times a year, Labor Day, Mother's Day, and Halloween.

Core aerifying, dethatching and power raking are useful lawn care activities. They help reduce soil compaction and thatch, improve surface drainage, and improve conditions prior to overseeding. These activities are best done when the grass is actively growing, and that's usually in spring or early to mid fall. The key right now is to complete the core aerifying, dethatching and power raking early enough in the fall for turf recovery to take place before the onset of severe cold weather.

Postemergence broadleaf weed control is suited to fall, too, especially for weeds such as dandelions, buckhorn, broadleaf plantains, and ground ivy. These weeds are preparing to go into dormancy for the winter. There is a lot of movement of materials within the plant and that's when herbicides work best to kill the entire plant.

When using any lawn or garden chemical, be sure to read, understand, and follow all label instructions for the safest, most effective application of herbicides. For more information, contact your local Extension office.

Keep Bugs Outside This Winter

Remember the ladybug invasion last year? Every year there seems to be some outbreak of critters that want in our home. In addition, mice will start coming in soon too.

Cooler weather prompts bugs and rodents to seek winter quarters. Often this results in their moving indoors with us. Spiders, millipedes, sowbugs, boxelder bugs, Asian lady beetles, and mice would all like to share your home with you this winter. Take time now, while the weather is still amenable, to prepare your home for this invasion.

Conduct fall-cleaning activities. Sweep spider webs away from windows and corners. Rake the accumulated leaves and grass away from the foundations. These activities eliminate hiding places, eggs, and easy access to your house by the pests.

The best way to keep critters out of your home is to prevent their entrance by caulking around windows and doors and at the top of the foundation. This will help keep out drafts, too. Be sure weather-seals at the bottoms of doors are tight. To keep mice from entering the house, cover all holes that are at least as big as the diameter of a lead pencil. Place ¼ inch wire mesh, smaller screening, or sheet metal around pipes and over ventilators or other holes.

A foundation spray might be helpful in extreme cases. Apply the diluted spray to the foundation for about three feet out from the house, and a foot or two up the side of the building. Remember though that the spray will only kill insects present during the spray and not those that come in later. If insects are not present already, do not use the spray. Again, I emphasize to read and follow all label directions carefully. Insecticides are hazardous to pets and humans, especially small children.

Most pests that do get indoors die in a few days. Boxelder bugs, ladybugs, and spiders may live indoors all winter. It is usually not advisable to spray them once they are in your home. The simplest way to eliminate them is to vacuum them up. Try not to crush boxelder bugs and ladybugs as they leave a stain and odor. These insects do not feed or reproduce indoors and are only seeking shelter. Spiders, on the other hand, will continue their normal habits, but only if they have insects on which they can live.

For mice, trapping is the most effective method of eliminating small numbers of mice, but sanitation is equally important. Store food in tight closing containers. Do the dishes daily and always wipe up crumbs from tables and counters. Remove nesting sites in garages and around the home or other buildings. When all else fails, trap or bait to control mice.

Leaves and Needles Everywhere

Fall colors are peaking now and are especially beautiful this year. Soon the leaves will fall and homeowners will start raking them, while children jump into the piles. It can be a fun time of year, but deciding what to do with all those leaves is often a challenge.

Since July 1, 1990, leaves and other landscape and yard wastes have been banned from Illinois landfills. Leaves are not a serious problem though since there are a variety of uses for them.

Leaves make excellent mulch for over wintering perennials or for beneath trees, shrubs, and other landscape plantings. If allowed to collect beneath the trees, leaves slowly decompose, releasing their nutrients to nourish the trees. This provides the litter that creates new, rich soil for tender roots. Large trees growing in the forest naturally have a layer of decayed leaves and leaf mold beneath them. This organic layer is the home of many beneficial organisms.

Of course, this does not work if there is grass beneath the trees, since the accumulated leaves will smother the grass. If there aren't too many leaves on the lawn, try grinding them with a power mower to let the tiny pieces fall between the blades of grass. A mulcher-mower does this especially well.

If you have room, a backyard compost pile provides an economical way to dispose of autumn leaves, while at the same time providing a source of organic nutrition for your garden. Leaves are an excellent material for compost. Composting is really very simple and a must for every home gardener. For more information on how to compost, contact your local Extension office. If you don't have or want your own compost pile, see if a neighbor will add your leaves to their pile. Or shredded leaves can be dug into vegetable or flower gardens in fall and will greatly improve the soil for next year.

Many people still burn leaves. Leaf burning is a controversial environmental issue. People suffering respiratory ailments often find that the air pollution caused by burning leaves aggravates allergic and asthmatic symptoms and makes breathing difficult. Many local governments prohibit or restrict leaf burning.

Use these tips to incorporate leaves into your landscape. It is the most ecologically sensible thing to do.

Naked Ladies

Naked Ladies are popping up all over. Naked Ladies are in full bloom right now. This beautiful flower goes by many common names including magic lily, resurrection lily, hardy amaryllis, and autumn amaryllis. The scientific name is *Lycoris squamigera* and it is in the Amaryllis family (close to the Lily family).

This lily is named as such because the leaves produced in the spring, die back to the ground by early summer, and then suddenly a beautiful pink flower reappears. The bright pink flowers are very showy and noticeable. However, since the leaves dieback the flower truly does look naked. Because of this, it is usually better placed at the back of the flower border or mixed with perennials that have good late-summer foliage. The wild flower garden and perennial border are possible choices for this 1 ½ to 2-foot tall flower.

The 3 to 4 inch flowers are lily-like and very fragrant. Flowers are usually pink, but can also be rose-lilac, white, or yellow. Usually there are 4 to 12 flowers atop the leafless stalk. Within the flower, the white filaments and yellow anthers are conspicuous, as with all lily-like flowers.

This plant is actually a bulb. Bulbs can be dug after the foliage dies in midsummer and the little offsets around the bigger bulbs should be transplanted immediately. Place the bulbs 5 to 8 inches apart and 4 to 6 inches deep. *Lycoris* grows well in full sun or partial shade in a well-drained soil. The soil should be dry during the dormant period.

As with all bulbs, make sure the leaves are completely brown and dead looking before removing them. As the leaves dieback, they keep producing food that is moved into the bulb. This food is needed for the best flower production and regrowth the following year.

There are other types of magic lilies available including *Lycoris radiata* (red spider lily) and *Lycoris sanguinea* (orange spider lily). However, these are listed for zones 7-10 and do not overwinter here. They would have to be moved indoors during the winter.

Ornamental Gourds

Last weekend I attended a wiener roast at a friend's home (Mark and Lynn Delost) in Canton. Mark had several decorative gourds there and asked me the name of one. I didn't know for sure because there are so many different types of gourds.

Gourds have been cultivated for thousands of years by many cultures worldwide. Found in Egyptian tombs were 4,000-year-old gourds. Pioneers and Indians used gourds for everything from musical instruments to cooking utensils, dishes, toys, and as ornaments.

Gourds are related to melons, squash, pumpkins, and cucumbers, all members of the Cucurbitaceae or Cucumber family. There are literally thousands of different gourd types. I will discuss two here: the cucurbita or ornamental gourds and the lagenaria or utilitarian gourds.

The cucurbita include the colorful, variously shaped ornamental gourds often used in fall arrangements. Plants of this group produce large orange or yellow blossoms that bloom in the daytime. This group contains most of the gourds we see this time of year, including those on the Spoon River Drive. They come in all shapes, sizes, and colors. Colors can be yellow, orange, green, white, or a combination of all. They can be striped, bicolored, or mottled. Shapes vary from fruits or eggs, to bottles, and beyond.

Ornamental gourds are often sold as small fancy gourd mix under the name *Cucurbita pepo*. There is such variation that it is really hard to pinpoint a specific type. Common names include apple, bicolor, crown of thorns, nest egg, orange, pear, and small spoon. Also sold as ornamental gourds are the larger Aladdin and Turk's Turban sold under the name *Cucurbita maxima.*

The lagenaria (*Cucurbita lagenaria*) group includes the utilitarian gourds such as the Martin or Birdhouse, Bottle and Dipper gourds. These plants produce white blossoms that bloom at night. Lagenaria gourds are green on the vine, turning brown or tan, with thick, hard shells when dry.

Popular in recent years are the penguin and swan types. Others are large gourds such as calabash, dipper, large bottle, bushel, and cucuzzi. Once dried and cured, these gourds can be used for a number of purposes for quite a long time.

For those who save seeds, the gourd types get even more interesting. Plants in this family will often cross-pollinate. Cross-pollination does not affect the current year's fruit, but will give interesting results the following year. Seeds saved from gourds grown in the garden will likely produce a cornucopia of fruit of different shapes, sizes and colors. Try it and have fun!

Overwintering Tropical Plants

Last weekend I brought in some of my tropical plants to overwinter. I want to save my banana, elephant ear, canna, mandavilla, coleus, and some other plants to use again next year.

Tropical plants are really popular in the landscape right now. Unfortunately in our midwestern landscapes, they are basically "one timers." They die quickly if exposed to freezing temperatures.

Fortunately, there are techniques to overwinter many of these plants thus saving you time and money by having the plants on hand when you need them next spring.

Instead of buying new each year, consider overwintering valuable specimens. The measures you take depend on the particular plant and its value as well as the facilities you have to successfully overwinter them.

There are five basic choices when it comes to overwintering tropicals: (1) overwinter the plant as a growing houseplant if you have proper conditions indoors; (2) store it as a dormant plant, tuber or root; (3) collect seed; (4) take cuttings or; (5) leave it outside in a protected location providing it with suitable mulch or covering.

Many tropicals can be overwintered as houseplants. Large specimen palms, bananas and ficus can be brought indoors and enjoyed so long as two requirements are met — high amounts of light and added humidity. Provide plants with the brightest location possible. Locate plants in high humidity areas if good light is available or group plants together. Grouping naturally raises the humidity in the vicinity. Expect some leaf loss when they are brought indoors from their outdoor location.

Many tropicals such as elephant ear, canna and caladium form bulbs, tubers or corms. When these plants die back, these underground structures can be dug and stored in a cool, dark place through the winter. The best time to dig the bulbs and tubers is after a light frost has killed the tops back. Trim the stems down to 4-6 inches and dig the plant up. Allow the tubers to dry slightly for a day or so before storing. Place the tubers in a crate or box with ventilation holes and bury the tubers in peat moss or wood shavings. Place the box in a cool (45-50 degree), dark area. Inspect the tubers regularly through the winter checking for rotting or excessive shrinkage. If tubers are drying out, add just a small amount of moisture to the peat.

I'm looking forward to enjoying my tropical plants indoors this winter. I'm sure they'll provide a bright, warm look to my home on a dark winter day.

Pawpaws

Last weekend my husband and I went camping in Southern Illinois with a group of friends. We hiked in Shawnee National Forest, did a little geocaching, and followed the wine trail. It was great fun!

While hiking the Little Grand Canyon, we passed several large groves of pawpaw trees. This beautiful native tree is usually found as an understory plant in cool, moist areas along streams. I first found it in my Mom and Dad's woodland along a little stream behind their house in Schuyler county.

The plant has many nice features. As a small understory tree, it only grows 15 to 20 feet tall and wide. It prefers moist, well-drained soils and will grow in shade to full sun. The large leaves are eye-catching, droopy and 6 to 12 inches long, and turn a beautiful golden yellow in fall.

Flowers are interesting as well. Looking like little 1 ½ inch purple bells along the stem, the flowers emerge from hairy, brown buds before the leaves in April and May. All buds on this plant have a silky, brown look and feel to them. Flowers turn into edible fruit that is two to five inches long and look like mangos or short, fat bananas. Animals love the tasty fruit, so they are often hard to find.

The fruit starts out green, then turns yellow, eventually ripening to brown or black. The unique flavor of the fruit resembles a blend of various tropical flavors, including banana, pineapple, and mango. The flavor and custard-like texture make pawpaws a good substitute for bananas in almost any recipe. Since I don't like bananas, I have never tried pawpaws. My parents have though and said they were so-so. They probably just needed the proper preparation technique.

The Kentucky State University Cooperative Extension Program has a large website on pawpaws. They say that the pawpaw is the largest edible fruit that is native to the United States and that most enthusiasts agree that the best way to enjoy pawpaws is to eat them raw, outdoors, picked from the tree when they are perfectly ripe. But there are also numerous ways to use them in the kitchen.

Now for some of the bad news. This plant is extremely difficult to transplant, so opt for small container-grown seedlings. It is virtually unattainable in the retail nursery trade, but can be obtained from specialty mail-order.

Another warning is that it does like to grow in groves. In *Dirr's Hardy Trees and Shrubs* book Michael A. Dirr says it "will sucker and produce colonies that make an almost eerie, enchanted-forest quality." Sounds like pawpaws would make a Halloween spook house setting!

Pumpkins

Pumpkins and autumn naturally go together. Those of you celebrating Halloween carve pumpkins into jack-o'-lanterns. Many of you, including my sister (Lynn Miller), simply enjoy decorating with uncarved pumpkins or eating pumpkin desserts.

Pumpkins are native to this country and have been immortalized in legend and history. They were obviously a vital source of food to the earliest settlers in this country. Pumpkins were made part of literature in the Legend of Sleepy Hollow.

Mostly, pumpkins are great for eating. They are used to make pumpkin butter, pies, custard, bread, cookies, and soup. The flowers may be picked just before or as they open, dipped in batter and fried as a delicacy. The small, immature pumpkin fruit (before the seed develops) may be prepared like a summer squash. These young, tender fruits may be steamed or boiled and then served as a buttered vegetable; or sliced, dipped in batter, and fried. The immature pumpkin is sometimes cut into strips and eaten raw with dips for snacks. The seeds of "naked-seeded" varieties do not have tough seed coats and can be roasted in the oven or sautéed for snacks.

There are many different varieties or types of pumpkins available. Small pumpkins are grown primarily for fall decorations or for cooking and pies and are usually referred to as "pie" types. They vary in size from less than 2 pounds to more than 5 pounds.

Intermediate and large varieties are used primarily for jack-o'-lanterns and decorating. Recent variety developments greatly strengthened the walls of these pumpkins so that much rounder, more attractive fruit are produced with fewer flat sides.

Processing pumpkins are a different species of pumpkins and are almost exclusively canned commercially. They have the familiar dark orange interior flesh, but look more like a buff-colored watermelons on the outside.

Jumbo or mammoth pumpkin varieties are again a different species. These attract much attention and have long been used for exhibits at county fairs. Winners routinely top a quarter ton. To grow a big pumpkin, genetics is everything. The better and larger the pumpkin your seed comes from, the better your chance of producing a whopper of your own.

There are many more types of pumpkins too including white varieties, long necked ones, and miniatures. Enjoy your pumpkins this fall. Uncut, they will last several months at about 50 degrees.

Reunion Gardens

Last Saturday was my Canton High School class reunion. My husband Mark and I both graduated from Canton High in 1981. The centerpieces at the reunion this year were rocks painted purple or gold to represent the painted rock in front of Canton High.

Reunion gardens use flowers in your school colors. You've probably noticed that school colors typically include bright, complementary colors. This also works to create dramatic gardens.

In the case of Canton, purple flowers are actually most vibrant when placed with their complementary color, yellow (or gold). Another option is to use chartreuse foliage with the purple flowers. There are purple foliages too, but they are usually more of a deep maroon color. Here are some examples of purple and gold plants to try.

Plant some bulbs this autumn for interest next spring. Many small flowering bulbs are available in shades of purple and gold such as crocus and anemone. Crocuses to consider include the purple 'Remembrance' and gold 'Yellow Mammouth.' For blue-purple accents add grape hyacinths or scillas. There are several tulips that could work such as 'Attila'.

There are many annual flowers that come in purple. For early spring color use a pansy in deep purple with a gold eye. Other purple annuals include petunia, verbena, gomphrena, ageratum, and statice. For gold annuals try marigolds, gaillardia, gerbera, nasturtium, or tithonia.

A nice perennial combination might be Salvia 'East Friesland' and Achillea 'Coronation Gold' or 'Parker's Variety'. Other perennials in purple include campanula, centaurea, and sage. For gold perennials try daylilies, coreopsis, or heliopsis.

Fall offers many options for the purple and gold garden. Asters and mums both come in many shades of purple. For example, the 'Violet Queen' aster has violet-purple daisies with a dark gold center. Mums are available in purple and gold. In fact, fall flower colors are typically more golden and thus work perfectly.

Obviously, there are many more options than I've listed here. I'll try a purple and gold garden in my yard next year. Maybe I should do an Illini garden in blue and orange as well!

Roadside Flowers

Have you noticed the beautiful flowers blooming along our roadsides right now? Illinois roadsides are quite beautiful in late summer.

Grass is the most obvious roadside plant. The unmown grass is in full bloom and appears graceful as it sways with the wind (or passing vehicle). Grasses make their peak in late summer, but are attractive even in winter when the golden, dead foliage creates a stunning presence in a stark landscape. Common grasses along roadsides include foxtails and fall panicum.

Bright yellow Jerusalem Artichoke makes a spectacular show this time of year. This sunflower has a yellow, three-inch flower and can grow five to ten feet tall. The Indians cultivated this large, coarse sunflower for its edible tuber. I sampled some of these pickled tubers recently at the *Illinois' Incredible Edibles* event at Dickson Mounds State Museum. They left quite a taste in my mouth!

Chicory and Queen Anne's Lace are two very common roadside features. Chicory has a bright blue, 1 ½ inch wide flower and grows one to four-feet tall. Only a few flower heads open at a time and each last only a day. The roots are sometimes used as a coffee substitute or additive. Queen Anne's Lace, also known as wild carrot, has lacy, flat-topped cluster of tiny cream-white flowers. Each flower has one dark flower at the center. It is the ancestor of the garden carrot.

Some roadside plants are not a welcome sight. I cringe whenever I see noxious weeds such as Musk Thistle or ragweed. Noxious weeds are plants that are required by law to be controlled. Unfortunately, we still see them everywhere. Musk thistle actually has a beautiful purple flower head, but it will quickly take over as it spreads. Ragweeds are noxious within towns because they cause severe allergies in some people. The culprit is pollen released by their inconspicuous green flowers.

Goldenrod is often mistaken as an allergy inducer because it blooms when ragweed pollen is abundant. There are many different types of goldenrod. They all have yellow arching flower heads and grow two to seven-feet tall. At a recent conference I learned a new goldenrod is now available for the perennial flower garden. It is *Solidago* x 'Crown of Rays' and gives quite a spectacular splash of yellow in the garden.

I hope this helps you better appreciate the roadsides you drive past each day. Please remember these cautions however: do not collect roadside plants and keep your eyes on the road for safe driving.

Salsa

Over the past decade, Americans have grown to love salsa, surpassing ketchup as a favorite condiment. While there are many variations, a basic salsa recipe includes tomatoes, peppers, onions, garlic, cilantro and tomatillos. I've made tomato salsa several times this summer from plants grown in my garden. You can too!

The type of tomato used will affect the thickness and quality of the salsa. Pasta tomatoes such as 'Roma,' Viva Italia,' and 'Veeroma' are firmer and produce a thicker sauce than slicing tomatoes. Slicing tomatoes, such as 'Big Boy,' 'Celebrity,' or 'Floramerica' yield a watery, thinner salsa.

Peppers vary greatly in taste and degree of heat. You can vary the hotness of the salsa by the peppers you use. Peppers used in salsa from mildest to hottest are Bell, Jalapeno, Cayenne, Thai and Habenero.

To get the largest garlic bulbs (*Allium sativum*) plant individual garlic cloves in well-drained soil in October. Plant 2 inches deep and mulch to prevent heaving in the winter. Garlic varieties to consider include 'New York White,' and 'German Extra Hardy.'

Cilantro (*Coriandrum sativum*) is easy to grow from seed. Plant seeds or transplants in full sun. Select varieties which are known for foliage rather than seed production, consider less flowering cultivar such as 'Santo.' Successive plantings are necessary to maintain a constant supply of cilantro.

Tomatillos, known as Mexican husk tomatoes, resemble green tomatoes with a husk. Remove the dry outer husk before using; they do not need to be peeled or seeded.

Homemade fresh salsa can be made to suit your taste buds. Rinse all the herbs and vegetables with water prior to peeling and chopping.

Soil Testing

Now is the time to take soil tests. Each year I test a different area so that all areas are tested every three to five years. Last year was the vegetable garden. This year I plan to test my orchard soil. My new fruit trees and brambles are not growing the way I would like them to. I suspect the whole area may need some soil amendments.

Lime and fertilizer recommendations can be no better than the sample tested. Be sure the sample is representative of the area to be treated. The teaspoon of soil finally used for analysis weighs a few grams in comparison to about 50,000 pounds of soil per 1000 square feet to a six-inch depth.

Before sampling the area, size it up for differences in soil characteristics, such as color, texture and drainage. If these features are uniform throughout the area to be treated, a single composite sample of the topsoil is adequate. If there is great variation in these features, take a composite sample from each predetermined area.

Soil samples may be taken at any time of the year when temperature (soil not frozen) and moisture conditions permit. Late summer and fall sampling is a good choice based on factors affecting nutrient availability and time available to the gardener.

Within the area selected for a sample, dig a hole to

spade depth. With a shovel or trowel cut a thin slice down one side of the hole. Place this slice in a pail or pan. Do not include sod roots. Repeat this procedure in at least eight well-scattered spots within the chosen area. Place each slice in the pail with those previously taken. Break up clods and mix the slices of soil thoroughly with the hands and by revolving the pail while held at an angle of 45 degrees. Use about one pint of the soil as a sample. Discard the remainder.

Soil testing and fertilizer application are only one step in effective soil management. For best growth of lawns, vegetables and ornamentals, you should also provide the proper soil structure and soil moisture. You can improve or maintain soil structure by working the soil properly and by incorporating organic matter into the soil. You can control soil moisture by improving drainage, by irrigating, and where practical, by applying mulches.

Spoon River Drive Scavenger Hunt

It is time for my annual Spoon River Drive Scavenger Hunt article in honor of the 39th Annual Spoon River Valley Scenic Drive. The goal of my scavenger hunt is to encourage readers to ignore the crowds and traffic jams and focus on our beautiful Spoon River Country.

So, this is simple and non-stressful. Look for the following 10 items as you participate in this year's drive. Some items you'll find sold in crafts and other items you'll find in the natural surroundings along the drive.

Bright red or sometimes orange leaves are seen on poison ivy and Virginia Creeper as they climb trees. Notice how the tree trunks look like they are wrapped with red brilliance.

Sugar maple treetops show variations of orange and yellow. These are some of the prettiest trees in the fall.

Ash trees turn a dark purple or bright yellow. While

looking at the trees, watch for local wildlife. You might see a squirrel in the treetops or a rabbit underneath. Watch for brightly colored birds such as cardinals and jays.

Sweetgum trees are not real common here, but might be seen planted in yards along the drive. Their leaves turn a variety of colors in the fall, ranging from yellow to orange to purple. Also look for crafts made from the sweetgum ball fruit of the tree.

You might find chestnuts for sale along the drive. Chestnuts look very similar to buckeyes, but have a slightly pointed end and are not as shiny. They are wonderful roasted or used in dressings.

Along road edges, you'll likely see the bright red leaves of sumac.

Pokeweed is eye stopping with its bright red stem and bright purple berries. Although a weed in most settings, it is quite a beautiful fall plant.

Goldenrod creates streams of gold and yellow among the roads and pastures of Fulton County. There are literally hundreds of different types of goldenrod in all sizes and shades of yellow. See if you can tell the differences among those you see.

Gourds come in all shapes and sizes. There are also many different colors of gourds, so pick your favorite to create a fall display.

Finally, choose your favorite Fulton County scene as you are driving along or stuck in traffic. The next time you have a bad day, picture that scene in your mind and relax. Although this scavenger hunt has no prize, you will find that you are blessed simply to be in beautiful Spoon River Country!

Spring Bulbs

Start next year's flower display this fall. This is the time to set out the spring flowering bulbs. It seems like a lot of work now, but after the long winter you will really enjoy those blooms. In addition to the standards such as tulips and daffodils, try some of the other small flowering bulbs. For example, anemones, snowdrops, and winter aconite all bloom very early and have especially beautiful flowers. Snowdrops are among the smallest and daintiest of the spring-flowering bulbs and often flower in early March, before all the snow has gone.

Bulbs can be planted in perennial borders, rock gardens, or naturalized in the lawn and wild flower garden. They are grown for beauty, fragrance, cut flower use, or combinations of these. The informal growth of plants such as daffodils adapt well to naturalized plantings, but also do well in small groupings or foundation plantings. Tulips, on the other hand, are very formal and look best when planted in clumps or beds of one color. Hyacinths provide colorful spring interest and fragrance.

Buy your bulbs early while the selection is good. Although late October is the best time to plant bulbs, anytime now will do. The ideal planting time is about four weeks before the ground freezes. This allows the bulb to grow some roots before winter. Select bulbs that are firm and free from soft or rotting spots or other signs of disease. Bulbs do best in well-drained soil. If your soil has a high clay content, the drainage can be improved by adding composts, peat moss, or other organic material.

To encourage root development this fall, many gardeners add phosphorus at planting time. The most common way to do this is to sprinkle a teaspoon of bone meal in the bottom of each hole, cover it with a little soil, and then place the bulb. You can also fertilize the shoots as soon as they break through the soil in the spring, but do not fertilize bulbs after flowering.

The most important part of bulb planting is proper depth. As a rule of thumb, plant the bulb two to three times as deep as it is wide. Large bulbs such as tulips and daffodils will be planted about 8 inches deep and smaller bulbs like crocus will be planted 3 to 4 inches deep. Measure planting depth from the bottom of the bulb. Bulbs should be planted with the nose of the bulb upward and the basal or root plate down. Special tools such as bulb augers for the drill and hand diggers are available. Use these if they work better for you, but many prefer to simply dig individual holes with a hand trowel.

Spend a little time this fall planting bulbs for great beauty next year.

GARDENING IN WINTER

African Violets

African violets are houseplants most people recognize. They are very popular and easy-to-grow. I bought two African violet plants last Saturday for my home. I haven't grown them for many years, but as a child I truly enjoyed them.

African violet (*Saintpaulia ionantha*) is a member of a large, interesting plant family known as Gesneriads. They are originally from tropical East Africa. As I always taught my University of Illinois students, it helps to understand where a plant comes from to better care for it. Picture an African violet in its native setting alongside tropical waterfalls and mountainous streams. Obviously, we cannot recreate a tropical waterfall in our homes, but we can give the plant what it likes most.

Proper water and light are key to growing African violets successfully in the home. Medium to high light is ideal. They do best with sun in winter and diffused bright light in summer. The plant will grow in lower light, but must have higher light in order to flower.

Irregular and excessive watering results in several problems. Proper, regular watering is important. This is the one plant I will water from the bottom because any water splashed on the leaves will spot and discolor the leaves. If watered from below, set the pot in a saucer of water, but remove as soon as moisture appears at the surface. You may want to give it a good top watering every few months to leach soluble salts from the soil. Do this by watering from the top until the water drains from the bottom a few seconds. Regardless of the watering method, always allow the soil surface to dry thoroughly between watering. Overwatering can be fatal to African violets.

Although these plants tolerate most home conditions, they do best at 70-80^0 with greater than 30% relative humidity levels. Trim off dead flowers. After flowering, plants rest briefly then reflower with adequate light. While not in flower, use general indoor plant fertilizer at half recommended strength every 3-6 weeks.

Repot only as needed to renew crowded or overgrown plants. It is best to use special African violet potting mix because it contains proper humus amounts. If your plant is very old and has a trunk-like stem, you might consider propagating a new plant. Simply cut off a leaf and stem and place it in a loose medium such as vermiculite or sand-mix. Thoroughly wet the pot and place it all in a clear-plastic bag near a window. When the cutting has rooted, a cluster of leaves will form at the base of the stem. Remove the plastic bag and you have a new plant! This really is easy to do. I propagated several plants as a child and gave them away. Two of my aunts still have those plants.

The Bald Eagle

My family has really enjoyed watching the bald eagles this winter. I find this especially awesome knowing that the eagles came very close to extinction. Now I know you wonder why I am writing about eagles in a gardening column, but there is a connection.

The bald eagle was originally classified as endangered in 1967. Shortly after World War II, the use of chemicals such as DDT and other related compounds (including Chlordane) became widespread. These chemicals last a long time in our environment and started to accumulate in bald eagles due to their natural feeding habits. The DDT impaired the eagles' eggs, resulting in thin eggshells and reproductive failures. Since that time, the US-EPA has banned such chemicals, and conservation and breeding efforts have brought our national bird population back.

I tell you this because I think it is a great story of how humans can fix a problem we created. Think of this story each time you use a pesticide. Pesticides are anything used to control a pest and include insecticides, herbicides, fungicides, etc. When you grab the ant killer under the kitchen sink, you are using a pesticide.

As homeowners, you too can apply pesticides in a safe and effective way that will obtain the control you want and still protect your family and our environment. You simply need to read the label. Reading the label is extremely important and it is the law! Labels change frequently, so you need to reread them each time you use the product. Carefully follow all directions on that pesticide label.

The label contains three basic types of information: product information, precautionary statements, and directions for use. You need to read it all. First, be sure the product is labeled for the intended use. For example, an outdoor ant spray cannot legally be used indoors and field corn herbicides cannot be legally used on garden sweet corn. Second, read the precautionary statements to find out potential hazards the product may have and how you should dress to protect yourself. In general, you should always have on long sleeves and long pants, with shoes and socks. Sometimes you might also need to wear impermeable gloves. Never get in a hurry and spray the lawn weeds while wearing shorts, tee shirt, and sandals. Finally, read the directions for use. It will tell you how to properly apply the product.

I spent the past 10 years working in pesticide safety education at the University of Illinois and therefore have strong feelings on this subject. Whether you use pesticides or not is a personal decision, but if you do (and most of us will), use them with respect and READ THE LABEL!

Christmas Cactus

With Thanksgiving behind us, most of us are gearing up for the holidays. Holiday plants help create the holiday spirit. Therefore, my next few Master Gardener articles will focus on holiday plants. Let's start off with Christmas cactus.

My mother says her Christmas cactus is absolutely beautiful this year, with blooms at the end of every branch. I would like to think my horticultural talents helped her achieve this wonderment, but actually she did it all on her own.

There are many different types of cacti that bloom between Thanksgiving and Easter. Each is appropriately named by the holiday it blooms near. The differences between these plants are found in the leaf edges. Christmas cacti have scalloped edges while Thanksgiving and Easter cacti have pointed edges. The Thanksgiving cactus is most common, probably because it is easier to get to bloom. They each are available in a variety of flower colors including white, pink, red, and orange.

When purchasing a new plant, look for uniform, green growth, and good flower bud set. While "cacti" usually suggest high temperatures and dry air, this is not what these holiday bloomers prefer. Unlike most cacti, these like moist soil and cooler temperatures. Take care of your flowering cacti much like you would any other houseplant. Give it a cool, sunny window or other location with bright, indirect light. Too much light can cause flower color to fade. Day temperature of 70°F and evening temperatures of 60-65°F are considered ideal. Avoid overwatering during flowering. Do not fertilize when plants are flowering.

The secret of getting your holiday cactus to bloom is one of air temperature. All of these cacti require a cool night temperature of about 60°F to bloom. Long nights are important too to get them to bloom. Mom started her blooming process by putting it outside all summer. This gave it ideal conditions to grow and flourish in preparation for the blooming season. Leave it outside as long as possible into the fall. If you must bring it in before October 1, leave it in a cool, light area of a basement or other area (Mom put hers in the garage). Remember, you must provide the plant a cool location with long nights. Bring it back to the cool, sunny window as soon as buds start to show.

If buds start to drop, it may be an indication of one of three things: the plant may need repotting, the temperature may be too high, or the light intensity too low. These plants seldom flower well at temperatures above 70°F.

If you don't have a holiday cactus, consider getting one this holiday season. They also make great gifts that, with proper care, will provide beauty for years to come.

Christmas Trees

There is nothing like the smell of a fresh Christmas tree to put you in the holiday spirit. The following tips may help you choose the perfect tree for your home and assure it stays fresh throughout the holiday season.

The first step to the perfect tree is selection. The most popular cut tree sold is the Scotch pine, but there are other types available too. Scotch pines are often locally grown and are usually cheaper than other types. Other common Christmas trees include Douglas fir, balsam fir, white fir, and my favorite the Fraiser fir. Fir trees make nice Christmas trees due to their shorter needles, but are usually considerably more expensive. Colorado blue spruce and other spruces typically do not make a good Christmas tree. White pine make beautiful Christmas trees, but the branches are soft and do not hold heavy ornaments well.

Whatever type you prefer, look for quality in the tree. It should be fresh, clean, well trimmed, and have good shape. The freshness of a tree is directly related to the moisture content of its needles. The best way to assure a tree is fresh is to cut it yourself or buy it from a reliable dealer. You can also test for freshness on the sales lot. Fresh trees have firm needles that are not brittle when grasped. (However, if temperatures are near zero, even a fresh tree will have brittle needles.) They will have a strong fragrance and good natural green color; however some trees are sprayed with a colorant. Shake the tree. If lots of outer green needles fall to the ground, it is probably too dry.

Once the tree is home, always re-cut the base and put the tree into a bucket of water. Although that fresh cut is often a hassle, it is necessary. Whenever the stem end of a fresh cut tree is exposed to air, a seal forms. The tree cannot take up water through that seal and will dry out. The only way to prevent the seal from forming is to make a fresh cut anytime the tree is taken out of water.

If you are not ready to bring the tree into the house, store it in a garage or outside away from winds. Once inside, expect a fresh-cut tree to use one-half to two gallons of water the first day. Check it several times the first day. Use a tree stand that holds plenty of water to assure your tree doesn't dry out. After the first day, the tree will use less water throughout the holiday season as it adjusts to the indoor environment.

Ideally, the trees should be displayed in a location out of direct sunlight and away from sources of heat or flame. If you must place the tree in one of these spots, make sure fresh water is provided every day.

It is not necessary to add anything to the water for your Christmas tree. Do not add aspirin, sugar, soda pop, or anything else to the water. All your tree requires is clear, cool, fresh water and lots of it.

Creating a Backyard Wildlife Habitat

My husband calls our yard a bird sanctuary this year. We do seem to have more birds than ever and they are a joy to watch. Apparently we must be doing something right to make our yard attractive to birds (and other wildlife).

Wildlife needs food, water, cover, and space. Every wildlife species has its own preferences and requirements for each of these elements. You might not be able to provide everything on your property. Look at neighboring land to see what plants are present, and allow them to complement the plants growing on your property.

Consider plant components for your yard. Evergreens provide shelter from the weather and predators. Spruce, cedar, pines, and other conifers also provide excellent nesting cover and are important in the winter to provide privacy all year.

Grasses and legumes also provide cover, food, and habitat for ground-nesting birds. Ornamental grasses, native wildflowers, clovers, or unmown areas of your yard will serve well.

Here are some plants that provide cover and food for birds. The American cranberry viburnum is excellent to attract cardinals and many other birds. The American Elder, or elderberry, has large flat white flower clusters in spring and purple to black fruit in late summer that attracts flycatchers, warblers, goldfinches, and 50 other species. Place the elder carefully though, as it is not a particularly pretty shrub. Hawthorns, crabapples, dogwood, and mountain ash are other good choices.

Consider adding plants that attract butterflies, bees, hummingbirds, and orioles. Plants that attract butterflies include aster, thistle, cosmos, marigold, yarrow, and of course butterfly bush and weed. Hummingbirds will go to bee balm, sage, impatiens, columbine, lily, phlox, and coralbells. Orioles feed on fruits, insects, nectar, and blossoms. We've had several orioles this year. They are not only beautiful, but have a wonderful song.

In addition to plants, consider non-living components, which can be as important as plants in providing good habitat for wildlife. In some instances, they are very easy to incorporate into your landscape. Examples include nest boxes, dead or fallen trees, brush or rock piles, dust or grit, salt, water, and finally feeders.

Many of you have birdhouses, feeders, and baths. Dead or fallen trees are like gold in the wildlife world. Many birds and other critters create cavities for nesting and perching sites. Without them, many species will move on. Dead branches, snags, and artificial perches will add to the use of your backyard habitat

Consider adding some of these elements to your yard this year. Then, sit back and enjoy the show!

Dormant Pruning

Now is the best time of year to do most pruning activities on your woody landscape plants. Deciduous trees and shrubs benefit from pruning this time of year. Light pruning may be done any time of the year, but heavy pruning usually should be limited to the latter part of the dormant season, preferable from February 1 to April 1. This is true for fruit trees as well.

Pruning does not have to be complicated or difficult if you follow these simple rules. First, and most important, never ever leave stubs. Always make cuts back to an existing branch or stem. It is important to position the cut adjacent to a bud where new growth will come from. Not doing this leaves stubs that often rot and can contribute to disease moving into the heartwood of the plant.

Second, cut out the 3-D's from the plant: diseased, dead, or damaged material. Remove dead or broken branches and diseased branches or branch parts. You can tell if a stem or branch is alive by slightly scratching it with a key or fingernail. If green shows through underneath the bark, it is alive. Once the 3-D's are removed, stand back and look at your work. Often times you are done at this point.

If you need to continue pruning, my third step is to remove suckers and watersprouts from the plant. Watersprouts are rapidly growing young shoots that grow straight out of the trunk or branch. They grow straight upward, frequently without branching. Remove these, as they are very weak wooded. Suckers arise from the roots or truck base. Remove these from single-trunked trees.

Again you might be done at this point. If not, next remove crossing branches that compete against each other. If one branch grows into another branch or rubs another branch, they can damage each other allowing an injury point for disease entry. Remove the least desirable branch or branch part.

Don't overdo it. Step back and look at your work often. If in doubt, leave it until the next time you prune. I like to prune a plant well about every three years or so.

Fruit trees are different in many ways, including pruning specifications. Fruit trees should be pruned a little every year. The first five years, prune fruit trees only enough to properly train the tree. Severe pruning can delay the development of bearing wood and thus, slow the onset of fruiting. If you have an overgrown older fruit tree, prune it slowly over 3-4 years to bring it back into production.

Proper, regular pruning of dead and diseased parts of a plant helps keep it strong, vigorous, and more resistant to storm damage.

Dried Flower Arrangements

Our new Ag Program Coordinator, Julia Pryor, brought in a flower arrangement this week to help decorate our annual office Thanksgiving dinner (we are starting the Thanksgiving eating early this year!). Julia's beautiful display reminds me that dried flower arrangements work well this time of year.

In addition to flowers, stems, and leaves that may be dried indoors, there are many materials that can be collected in the fall and used almost directly in arrangements after gathering. These include many seedpods, cones, grains, grasses, and berries found in the garden, as well as in fields and along roadsides.

Berries add great color and texture to an arrangement.

Rosehips are a great example. This somewhat spherical fruit of the rose, usually red in color, is seldom allowed to develop on our modern roses. However, the old-fashioned shrub types, such as the rugosa, bear them abundantly. The rugosa rosehips are large (1/4 inch) and bright red.

Other berries to try include cotoneaster, crabapple, bittersweet, hawthorn, euonymus, firethorn, viburnums, and more.

Interesting stems and twigs add texture and height to an arrangement. Curly stemmed plants work well for this. Examples include contorted hazelnut and corkscrew willow. Uniquely shaped stems of any kind will work.

Grass flower heads add softness. If you have ornamental grasses, these work great. You can also use the "weedy" grass flower heads that are abundant in our landscape. Examples you might look for include Bristly foxtail, Fountain grass, Northern sea oats, Pampas grass, Plume grass, Quaking grass, Spike grass, and Squirrel-tail grass.

Grains such as wheat, oats, rye, or even sorghum work well too. Other seedpods to try include poppy, lotus, cattail, dock , honesty (money plant), iris, lily, milkweed, mullein, Queen Anne's lace, and teasel.

You might still find some old flower heads in some gardens that are useable. These might include baby's breath, bachelor's button, bells of Ireland, cockscomb, globe amaranth, larkspur, scarlet sage and blue sage, sea lavender, statice, strawflower, and yarrow (yellow varieties best).

I encourage you to make a table decoration for your Thanksgiving table this year. Gather natural items and make a dried arrangement or purchase some fresh flowers to go with it. For a more traditional look, put the plant materials in a cornucopia or flat basket. Have fun and enjoy!

Ferns

You have probably noticed that many traditional houseplants are now sold as annual hanging plants. One common example is the Boston fern. I had two big, beautiful ones this summer hanging in my gazebo. Unfortunately, I did not have a place to move them inside and will need to buy new ones next spring.

The Boston fern is actually a mutation of the sword fern that was found near Boston in the 1890's. It soon became a fixture of the overstuffed parlors of the time, but later became known as an old fashioned plant. In the past twenty years, it has regained popularity. Today it has many uses including specimen pedestals, accent for tables, baskets, contrast for dish gardens or group plantings, and indoor groundcovers.

The Boston fern (*Nephrolepis exaltata* 'Bostoniensis') has graceful, arching fronds up to 3 feet long with flat 3- to 4-inch closely set leaflets. In addition, there are a number of mutations with different frond types. 'Bostoniensis' is more graceful and drooping than other varieties. 'Fluffy Ruffles' is a smaller plant, which grows more erect than other varieties. It has dark green fronds that grow about 12 inches long. The foliage has a finely ruffled appearance. 'Dallas' is also a smaller, compact plant with a curlier leaf. It is also tolerant of lower light and lower humidity.

As with all houseplants, proper water and light are key to success in the home. Medium to high light is ideal. They do best with sun in winter and diffused bright light to partial shade in the summer. Gradual yellowing and decline usually indicate poor light. Move the plant or prune away shade-producing vegetation.

As with most ferns, the Boston fern prefers a humid environment. This is hard to achieve in most homes. Because the plant is sensitive to chlorine and other chemicals often found in tapwater, regular misting is generally not recommended. Try to keep the soil moist at all times, but not soggy. The plants can be allowed to dry out between waterings if not excessively fertilized. Remember there is a fine line between moist and soggy. This plant's foliage and roots rot in wet conditions.

Other maintenance tips include cutting older fronds back to soil level to encourage fresh new growth. General grooming of brown leaflets is desirable. If you prefer to fertilize, use a general indoor plant fertilizer at one-quarter recommended strength every 4-6 weeks. This plant can take being root-bound, so repot infrequently.

Finally, place your Boston fern where people are not tempted to touch the fronds. Fronds will not tolerate being handled and will turn brown.

Frankincense and Myrrh

As I was deciding what to write for this Christmas column, my colleague Kevin McGuire suggested the title, "Just what is myrrh anyway"? We joked a bit about it and then I realized that he was right. Since both are plant products, an article on frankincense and myrrh is the perfect Christmas article. We all know the story of the Three Wise Men bringing gold, frankincense and myrrh to Baby Jesus, but do we really know what those products are and why they were so valuable?

Frankincense and myrrh are both resins -- dried tree sap -- that come from trees of the genus *Boswellia* (frankincense) and *Commiphora* (myrhh), which are common to Somalia and Ethiopia.

The value of these products comes partly from their use, but also from the labor-intensive way that they are harvested. To collect the tree's sap, the tree's bark is cut, causing the sap to ooze from the cut. The sap used to create both frankincense and myrrh comes slowly and is allowed to dry on the tree for several months. The hardened sap is collected and used as frankincense and myrrh.

Frankincense is used mainly for it's lovely fragrance, although historically it also had medicinal uses. Frankincense is a leafy tree that grows without soil along the rocky shores of Somalia. The young trees furnish the most valuable gum - a milky white ooze that hardens to a translucent golden hue.

Myrrh is collected from a small five to 15 foot tall tree about one foot in diameter called the dindin tree. The tree looks like a short flat-topped Hawthorne tree with gnarly branches. The whitish-green flowers appear before the leaves in the spring. The plant looks scrubby and desolate among the rocks and sands of the desert.

True myrrh is crumbly and dark red inside. The exterior is white and powdery. The best myrrh has little odor and no oily texture. High quality myrrh demanded the best prices in the Roman Empire, but it did not ship well.

The most common use for frankincense and myrrh – past and present – is as incense. Myrrh is also used medicinally, as an embalmer, in cosmetics, and today myrrh is found in some flavorings.

Today, you can find frankincense and myrrh for sale at stores and on the internet. Beware that the product you purchase may actually be resin from another Middle Eastern tree and not the real stuff.

Merry Christmas! I wish you all wonderful times with your family during this Holiday Season.

Garden Gifts

Are you searching for the "perfect" gift for a gardener in your family? Here are some ideas that might prove helpful. Gardeners always love gift plants and flowers. Since gardeners tend to be choosy about the type of plants they grow, get them a gift certificate to their favorite nursery. Or, give them a monthly subscription to receive fruit or plants each month for the next year.

All gardeners love gardening books and magazines. Give them a gift certificate for a substantial amount from any bookstore or online bookseller for the purchase of gardening-related books. Or, give them a gardening magazine subscription.

For gardeners who love jewelry, fun garden themed jewelry is a great gift. Pins shaped like a garden rake or shovel or flower necklaces are good ideas for women. For the male gardener, purchase a bird feeder, chimes, or other garden accessory.

Purchase gifts that will help the gardener avoid environmental hazards. All gardeners should use sunscreen, hats, sunglasses, gloves, proper shoes, long sleeved shirts and long pants, and ear protection when needed.

They must have a good pair (or two) of gardening gloves. I have three or four different types on hand to match the type of gardening I'm doing. Gloves protect hands from twigs, spikes, thorns or even the drying soil. Make sure they fit or they won't be worn.

Along with gloves, a gardener needs a good pair of gardening shoes, boots, or clogs. Clogs are often preferred because they are easy to slip on and work well for light gardening. Other gardening tasks require good sturdy shoes or boots.

For the indoor gardener, there are many options as well. A table top terrarium is a lovely way to grow and enjoy an indoor garden. Be sure to give them some little houseplants and soil to get the terrarium started.

A canvas tote filled with gardening supplies is great for the indoor or outdoor gardener. For indoor gardeners include perfectly sized tools, a plant mister, a light meter, and a good houseplant book. For the outdoor gardener include tools, pruners, string, plant tags, and gloves.

Finally, what could be better than a whole basket full of gardening treasures! A collection of garden delights might include green tea, natural snacks, and gardening essentials such as gardening gloves, hand tools, kneeling pad and jiffy-pots for seedlings.

Happy shopping! Oh, and if you are the gardener, cut out this article and leave it in an obvious spot for your loved one to see and get the hint!

Garden Planning

Last weekend I was in the garden-planning mood. I looked through some of my gardening books and surfed the internet for ideas. Already, my mind is swirling with ideas for my new yard! Do you need some inspiration? Here are some suggestions to get you started.

Check out your local library or visit a bookstore for gardening books. One of my favorites is *Creating a Family Garden* by Bunny Guinness, which gives great ideas on creating different outdoor rooms for the family including playrooms, workrooms, entertaining rooms, and more. My boys also enjoyed looking through the book and are developing the "perfect" treehouse. University of Illinois Extension offers a series of four publications on plants for the Midwest covering needled evergreens, ground covers, dwarf shrubs, and large flowering shrubs. This set provides great landscaping ideas to help you choose the right plant for the right place. Magazine articles and "how-to-do-it" books can also help generate ideas.

If you have a computer with internet capability, check out www.prairienet.org/garden-gate/ This site is maintained in Champaign, IL and contains areas for questioning, additional links, gardening newsgroups, gardening chat sessions, and more. The Teaching Garden lists by category many different sites on the internet. Think about what you are looking for and try to narrow your focus while using the internet. Otherwise it can become overwhelming and time consuming. For example, are you looking for garden design, plant selection, plant care, garden problem solvers, gardening software, reviews of gardening books, or a live chat session about gardening?

Another good source of gardening ideas is seed and plant catalogs. Many of these catalogs are very well done, with great pictures, and make great planning tools. My favorites include Parkseed, Burpee, Stark Bros, and White Flower Farm.

Attend a garden show or gardening program this winter.
Take a gardening program this winter from your local
Extension office.

Once you are inspired and have your own ideas "swirling
in your head," it is a good idea to organize those thoughts and
develop a plan. Landscaping is not merely the craft of growing
plants or building structures—it is the art of developing space
around your house for convenience, beauty, and pleasure.
So, spend some time this winter dreaming of your perfect
landscape. Then, develop your own long-term plan, establish
a budget, and with time you'll achieve that dream.

Green Plants Improve our Health

St. Patrick's Day reminds us all to look for green. Green
is the color of peace and serenity and important for our
psychological well being. Plants play a big role in filling that
psychological need. Much research has been done on the
importance of plants in our lives.

Have you ever noticed how people choose seats next to
plants when given a choice in malls or parks? Our world
is busy and we are constantly bombarded with noise,
movement, and chaos. Plants help relax us. Because of their
simplicity, plants, or natural scenes, reduce physical and
mental excitement and improve our health.

Research has found that in offices with plants, employees
are more content and comfortable. Plants in an office result
in higher office morale and less absenteeism. Employees
exposed to plants were more creative and productive. This,
in part, is why you find plants in most business settings
and other interior settings. The federal government has
strongly endorsed the use of plants as an integral part of
office interiors.

As St. Patrick's Day approaches, remember how important
plants are to our psychological well being. A popular St.
Patrick's Day plant is the shamrock. Although there are
several types available, the most popular is the Oxalis due

to its shamrock leaves. The leaves are in threes, with each individual leaflet 1 ½ to 2 inches wide. Available with purple or green leaves, this plant is easily grown for table tops or hanging baskets. An added plus is the white or pink flowers that open in winter and spring and continue all year round with sufficient light.

The shamrock plant is actually a bulb or tuber. After flowering, leaves may die down and the tubers benefit from rest in drier soil and cooler temperatures. As new growth resumes, move it back to a warmer location, increase watering, and resume fertilizer applications. The plant prefers bright light without direct sun.

At times I have seen other plants sold as shamrocks. These include ordinary lawn clovers, weedy oxalis plants, and other clovers. However, the shamrock described above is the only one that makes a nice, long-term houseplant.

Another good green St. Patrick's Day plant is the green carnation. These are actually white carnations dyed green. Use them in a vase or as a corsage. These are usually readily available this time of year. If not, you can easily dye a carnation green by letting it drink green colored water. White flowers can also be painted green with special floral paint.

Happy St. Patrick's Day!

Herbs and Spices

My Christmas dinner this year includes the traditional turkey and dressing. For dessert we'll have pumpkin and a fruit pie, plus more. My dinner will include a variety of herbs and spices, which make the food taste great!

What is the difference between an herb and a spice? Definitions of herbs and spices vary somewhat but can be identified as follows.

Herbs are leaves of low-growing shrubs. Examples are parsley, chives, marjoram, thyme, basil, caraway, dill, oregano, rosemary, savory, sage and celery leaves. These can be used fresh or dried. Dried forms may be whole, crushed, or ground. Many herbs can be grown in the United States in or out of doors.

Spices come from the bark (cinnamon), root (ginger, onion, garlic), buds (cloves, saffron), seeds (yellow mustard, poppy, sesame), berry (black pepper), or the fruit (allspice, paprika) of tropical plants and trees.

Sage is one of my favorite herbs. It can be used a variety of ways. I particularly like sage in dressing. You can also use it in meatloaf, soup (my Mom makes a great bean soup that takes sage!), bread, sausages, omelets, and more.

Sage is really easy to grow and a very pretty plant. It comes in a variety of leaf colors, including the traditional green. There is also purple sage, tricolor (cream, purple, and green), pineapple, golden, and more. Sage also has a beautiful purple flower that hummingbirds will visit.

I love pepper. I'm one of those people who pepper almost all my food. Black pepper comes from the pepper (*Piper nigrum*) vine in tropical locations. The black pepper is obtained from the dried unripe fruit. When the outer covering is removed it produces white pepper. To get green pepper, the green peppercorns are treated to retain the green color. Pink pepper or red peppercorns are rare and consists of ripe red pepper berries preserved in brine and vinegar. You can commonly find dried "pink peppercorns", but they are usually the fruits of a plant from a different family.

Paprika is a spice of the pepper plant. In the United States, paprika is typically made of non-pungent red chile peppers. In Europe, however, you can get paprika of varying degrees of "hotness" depending on which pepper was ground. Similarly, chili powder is made of ground peppers and is typically mildly spicy in the United States. Paprika and chili powder can be made from any pepper (*Capsicum* sp.) including the chili, cayenne, and red pepper.

Merry Christmas everyone! Enjoy this holiday season of good food with family and friends!

Holly and Mistletoe

Holly and mistletoe are symbols of the Christmas season. My son Derek noted the differences while we were decorating last weekend. They are very different plants, but both quite beautiful in their own unique ways.

Mistletoe is actually quite a pest in the South. It is most often found in the South, although it is occasionally found in Southern Illinois. It is a semi-parasitic plant that attaches itself to deciduous trees and "feeds" from that tree, although it also produces its own chlorophyll. The scientific name for mistletoe is *Phoradendron*, which in Greek means a thief ("phor") of a tree ("dendron"). Mistletoe in deed gets at least some nourishment from the trees on which they grow.

The sticky fruits are poisonous to man, but some birds can eat them. One or two berries are sufficient to cause severe poisoning or even death in a child. Therefore, any mistletoe you buy should have fake berries. This is definitely a time when artificial is okay. I tease that the sign of a good horticulturist is to know when and how to properly use fake plants!

From the earliest times mistletoe has been one of the most magical, mysterious, and sacred plants of European folklore. It was considered a bestower of life and fertility; a protectant against poison; and an aphrodisiac. Kissing under the mistletoe is first found associated with the Greek festival of Saturnalia and later with primitive marriage rites. For those who wish to observe the correct etiquette: a man should pluck a berry when he kisses a woman under the mistletoe, and when the last berry is gone, there should be no more kissing!

Holly is overall a much prettier plant. The deep, green holly leaves are shiny and spectacular. Their unique shape is found on many Christmas items, including cookie cutters. The red berries are also quite nice.

There are many different types of holly plants, but many are not winter hardy here. The most common holly grown in northern gardens is the Meserve Hybrid Hollies (*Ilex x meserveae*). Holly plants are either male or female. Both must be present in the near vicinity to ensure the female flowers and thus produce fruit. Generally we recommend planting one male plant to several female. To assure this, you must purchase your plants from a reputable source because there is no positive way to identify the different sexes until they flower.

Probably the best known of the holly trees grown in the United States is the American Holly. These are beautiful dense pyramidal evergreen trees. They are quite popular in Southern Illinois where they are more winter hardy. If male and female trees are within 2 city blocks, they produce beautiful berries that last all winter.

Literature Gardens

Have you ever thought of combining literature and gardening? Two gardens at the 1999 Chicago Flower & Garden Show did just that. Two popular children's books came alive in gardens: "The Tales of Peter Rabbit" and "Where the Wild Things Are."

One of the most popular (and crowded) gardens at this year's show was Mr. McGregor's Garden. In it the famous adventures of Peter Rabbit seem to come alive. Created by Craig Bergmann's County Garden in Winthrop Harbor, this exhibit focused on the young rabbit's escapades in Mr. McGregor's vegetable garden. As we walked around the outside of the garden, we read the story on strategically placed signs.

The story of Peter Rabbit was written by Beatrix Potter in 1902, but is still as magical today. The garden version included bits and pieces from the story. Peter's lost red jacket lay in the walkway, as did his shoes. Peter even made an appearance in the potting shed, hidden in a large watering can! This exhibit also included Mr. McGregor's carefully tended cottage flower garden of delphinium, foxgloves, clematis, bellflowers, roses, and sweet peas. The plant list for this garden included 5 trees and shrubs, 36 perennial flowering plants and vines, 6 different roses, 26 seasonal plants, 18 herbs, and 36 fruit and vegetable varieties. Quite an outstanding exhibit!

The other storybook garden was based on the popular children's book by Maurice Sendak called "Where the Wild Things Are." Although this garden could not as easily be created in a typical yard, it was still inspiring. This exhibit was crafted by Barbara's World of Geneva. Visitors explored a forest filled with life-sized woodland animal topiaries, including a six-and-a-half-foot bear. The topiaries were made of wire bent into animal and human shapes, which were covered with a sphagnum peat moss material. Large balled-and-burlapped trees were brought in to create the forest. The tallest plants were a backdrop of 10-15 foot bamboo. This was a magical garden as well!

Consider creating a literature garden in your own yard this summer. Base it on your own favorite book. Those that come to mind include "The Secret Garden," "Winnie the Pooh," "Charlotte's Web," and "Thumbelina," just to name a few. Obviously, they do not have to be as elaborate as those created in Chicago's Navy Pier for this show. A small corner of the yard would work just as well and be a great place to escape into a fairytale world.

Mother-In-Laws Tongue

Last weekend I cleaned and moved some of my houseplants. I have a rather large Mother-in-Laws Tongue that I cleaned and moved to the kitchen. I really like it there. This is a truly nice specimen plant that I've had since I was a kid.

Anyone can grow this plant – really! The Mother-In-Laws Tongue (*Sansevieria trifasciata*), also known as snake plant, is one of the most durable houseplants. It is extremely easy to grow, tolerates neglect and a wide range of temperatures. I don't know how it got the name Mother-In-Laws Tongue, but for me a great plant is named for a great lady. Like the plant, my mother-in-law (Barb Bohanan) is dependable and always there to provide cheer on a cloudy day.

This plant has tall, upright clusters of stiff leaves. Although many varieties are available, most have broad crossbands of grayish-green that decorate dark green foliage. The height is usually 3 to 4 feet. Cultivars offer different color variations and heights.

Most people grow either the tall green one or the cultivar 'Laurentii'. 'Laurentii' has yellow margins along the edges of the tall leaves. Other cultivars include 'Hahnii', the birds-nest sansevieria that grows only 4 to 8 inches tall, or 'Moonglow' that has leaves of creamy silver-green.

Last year my snake plant flowered. What a great surprise for me since I had never had one flower before. Only mature plants will flower. The flower is on a tall spike with white to green fragrant blossoms. They lasted quite a long time.

This plant will grow almost anywhere, but ideal conditions are as follows. They will tolerate most light conditions from very low dark areas to full sunlight. This plant prefers dry soil and does need to dry out between watering. They have very few pest problems.

The plant is also easy to propagate. Simply divide your larger plant into two smaller ones. Leaf cuttings can be taken too. Slice the leaves cross-wise into 2 inch long pieces and place in moistened soil to root.

As an added bonus, this plant is reported effective in tests to freshen or purify air. The *Foliage for Clean Air Council* has documented living plants' ability to absorb chemicals in the air such as tobacco smoke, and chemicals released from carpet, paint, and furnishings. Some plants can remove as much as 85 percent of certain common pollutants. As few as one efficient plant for every one hundred square feet can make a healthy difference to indoor air quality.

Put a snake plant in your house today. If you already have one, pull it out of the corner, clean it up and enjoy it even more.

Poinsettias

The Poinsettia is the traditional Christmas flower. It was introduced to the United States in 1825 by Joel Robert Poinsett, first U. S. ambassador to Mexico who obtained plants from the wilds of southern Mexico. Since the early 20th century, the Ecke family from California has become synonymous with poinsettias in the greenhouse industry. Almost all plant royalties for poinsettia cultivars are paid to the Ecke family and, chances are, your poinsettia spent time at the Ecke Poinsettia Ranch just north of San Diego.

The colorful parts of the Poinsettia are actually modified leaves called bracts. The real poinsettia flower is the small yellow "ball" in the middle of the colored bracts. The real flowers are petal-less and often fall off indoors due to low humidity and light levels. Poinsettias are available in many colors in addition to the traditional red, including pink, white, and many multi-colored varieties such as 'Jingle Bells' and 'Marble'.

When purchasing a poinsettia, look for two main features: dark green foliage and tight, intact "real" flowers. Avoid plants with yellow or damaged leaves because this could indicate poor handling, old plants, or a root disease problem. Tight "real" flowers indicate the plant is in an early stage and will last a long time. Once you choose the right plant, be sure it is well wrapped when you take it outside for your trip home. Even short exposure to low temperatures can injure leaves and bracts.

Once home, unwrap the plant as soon as possible. The best location for it is near a sunny window or other well-lighted area. A window that faces south, east or west is better than one facing north. Do not let any part of the plant touch the cold windowpane because this may injure it.

Proper watering is important. Examine the soil daily, and when the surface is dry to the touch, water the soil until it runs freely out the drainage hole in the container. Discard the water that collects in the outer foil wrap or saucer. Do not leave the plant standing in water. Overly wet soil lacks sufficient air, which results in root injury.

Poinsettias prefer temperatures between 60-70°F. They do not tolerate warm or cold drafts so keep them away from radiators, air registers, and fans as well as open windows and doors. To extend the blooming time further, place your poinsettia in a cooler location at night.

Finally, please be sure to note and tell your friends that poinsettias are not poisonous. Extensive laboratory testing and university research has concluded that poinsettias are not poisonous. However, this does not imply that they are edible. In addition, some people develop a dermal reaction (skin rash) if exposed to the white, milky sap of poinsettias.

Snow, Cold, and Plants

Sure looks like we'll have a white Christmas this year. The snow is pretty, but are you worried about the effects of snow and cold on your landscape plants? Fortunately, most of our landscape plants are well adapted to the snow and cold.

Accumulations of snow can cause severe damage to some landscape plants. Evergreens such as yews, hemlocks, and junipers are especially susceptible to damage from snow. Although wet snow is more hazardous to plants than drier powder snow, any heavy snow can cause problems. Increased weight from snow can cause branches of trees and shrubs to break. Therefore, if you notice your plants weighted down by snow, shake them off as soon as possible with a broom or light rake. Most plants will recover after the weight is relieved, but some could experience longer lasting injury.

Snow is typically safer on plants than ice. The right weather conditions can cause ice to coat all parts of plants, making them very heavy and susceptible to breakage. If ice develops do not attempt to remove it. Ice must melt away naturally. Pruning may be required if breakage does occur. Trees most susceptible to ice damage include those that are topped and those with weak forks and brittle wood such as silver maple, tree-of-heaven, mulberry, and willow.

Cold temperature effects on plants depend largely on the plant itself. Each type of plant has a different inherent tolerance to cold temperatures. Currently our outdoor plants are dormant and resting for the winter. Dormancy allows plants to withstand low temperatures. For example, a Norway maple tree can withstand a temperature of -30^0F when dormant but may be severely damaged by a temperature just below freezing during the growing season. However, even dormant plants can still suffer during the winter. Extremely cold winter temperatures usually do not kill entire plants, but can kill other parts such as flower buds of some marginally hardy plants including peaches and dogwood.

Heavy snows and cold temperatures in December can actually help to reduce overall plant damage. Heavy snows insulate the ground and therefore protect low-growing plants and roots from the cold. Roots never really go dormant and cannot tolerate low temperatures like aboveground parts can. Although the top of a boxwood shrub may be able to tolerate -10^0F, the roots will probably be killed at 20^0F. Snow cover is excellent mulch and helps keep roots warm. Snow cover also reduces the likelihood of frost heaving of plants.

Unfortunately, there really is little we can do to protect our landscape plants from cold temperatures. It is a wait-and-see situation. We'll find out this spring if significant damage occurred or not. The best way to prevent winter injury is to plant winter-hardy plant material and care for it properly.

Spirited Plants

Happy New Year! Where did 2004 go? My family typically toasts in the New Year with sparkling grape juice. Others will toast with spirited drinks. Whether you imbibe or not, it is interesting to think of all the plants that make up spirits.

Spirits are actually named by the fermented material from which they are distilled. Various grains make up whisky, vodka, gin and most types of schnapps. Brandy is made from fermented grape juice, and fruit brandy is made from other fruits. Rum and cane spirits come from fermented sugar cane juice or molasses. Tequila and mezcal come from the fermented pulp of the agave plant.

Whiskey is distilled from various grains. It is aged, often for long periods of time, in wooden barrels (usually oak), which adds aroma, flavor, and an amber hue. After some time, these whiskey barrels are cut in half and sold as plant containers. Scotch and Irish whiskies are made from barley, while North American whiskies are typically a mix of corn, rye, wheat, barley and other grains in different proportions.

Vodka is distilled from a mash of pale grain or vegetable matter, including potatoes, molasses, beets, and a variety of other plants. Rye and wheat are the classic grains for vodka, with most Russian vodkas being made from wheat. In Poland they are mostly made from a rye mash.

Gin is a juniper berry-flavored grain spirit. Junipers are grown worldwide and are very common foundation plants.

Rum comes from sugarcane. While touring the Bacardi factory in the Bahamas, I found out that Bacardi rum's special recipe is not only a distillation of molasses and water, but also special yeast. The yeast is the secret and has been growing since 1862.

Distilling the fermented juice of agave plants in Mexico makes tequila. The agave is a spiky-leafed member of the lily family (it is not a cactus) and is related to the century plant.

Other alcoholic beverages include wine and beer. Wine comes from grapes and other fruits, while beer is brewed from grain and hops.

For those of you who toast in the New Year with champagne, you might actually be drinking sparkling wine. Champagne is a region of France, and only wines that come from this region can properly be called "Champagne". Similar drinks from California and the rest of the world should be called "sparkling wines".

Have a safe and happy New Years! Please take care of yourself and each other and don't drink and drive!

Sugar

Last weekend my husband Mark and I were in the Bahamas. While there, we toured a Bacardi rum factory. Since rum is made from molasses, this got me to thinking about sugar products that we often use in baking during the holidays.

The sugar we use comes from two different plants: sugar beets or sugarcane. Worldwide, 70 percent of our sugar comes from sugarcane. Sugarcane is a tall grass that grows in tropical areas. I've seen it growing in Hawaii and Jamaica and the fields look similar to corn.

To get sugar from sugarcane, the cane is pressed to extract the juice, then boiled, and spun to produce raw sugar and syrup (molasses). The raw sugar is then sent to a refinery where it is washed and filtered to remove remaining non-sugar ingredients and color. It is then crystallized, dried and packaged into refined (or granulated) sugar.

To get confectioners (or powdered) sugar for icings and baking the granulated sugar is ground to a smooth powder, and contains about 3% cornstarch to prevent caking.

Molasses comes from the sugarcane extraction process. The quality of molasses depends on the maturity of the sugar cane, the amount of sugar extracted, and the method of extraction. There are three major types of molasses: unsulphured, sulphured and blackstrap.

Many restaurants now have packets of "Sugar in the Raw" with their other sweeteners. This is Turbinado sugar, which is a raw sugar that has been partially processed, removing some of the surface molasses. It is a blond color with a mild brown sugar flavor and is often used in tea.

Brown sugar consists of sugar crystals coated in molasses syrup. Dark brown sugar has more color and a stronger molasses flavor than light brown sugar.

Most of the sugar we eat here probably came from sugar

beets. Sugar beets are a root crop resembling a large parsnip grown mostly in the north. Beet sugar processing is similar to sugarcane, but it is done in one continuous process without the raw sugar stage. The sugar beets are washed, sliced, and soaked in hot water to separate the sugar-containing juice from the beet fiber. The sugar-laden juice is purified, filtered, concentrated and dried in a series of steps similar to cane sugar processing.

Did you ever know that sugar could be so complicated, yet taste so good? As you are eating holiday sweets, think about all the hard work people did to grow and produce that sugar product.

The Winter Garden

Don't let freezing temperatures and snow keep you cooped up indoors this winter. Winter is a wonderful time to explore plants outside in the landscape. Without their camouflage of summer leaves, the starkness of trees and shrubs during the winter season is most revealing.

Look for plant silhouettes. Each plant displays a branching silhouette characteristic only to that particular species. Branching habits range from strongly upright and horizontal to weeping and cascading. The bare silhouette of a big old tree looks very magnificent against the wintry sky.

Winter is also a good time to see different colors. The evergreens each come in a specific shade of green. It is really very amazing how many different greens are created in nature. Greens range from gray to blue to yellow and all shades in between.

Textures and patterns come alive in winter as well. Tree bark is of particular interest. Often tree bark is more striking during winter. Bark patterns are unique to each tree species and are often used in winter identification. The greenish, gray of an elm is quite different from a black, dark linden.

Also take a closer look at plant buds, seeds, seed capsules, and fruit. Some tree species have very unusual buds. For example, a flowering dogwood flower bud is usually at the end of stems and shaped like a flattened biscuit. In addition to buds, notice berries and fruits. Bright red berries come alive when they are no longer hidden with leaves. Even brown fruits like the Alder's small winged nutlets are beautiful as they persist through the winter.

In addition to the trees and shrubs, I particularly like the look of perennials and ornamental grasses in winter. If they were not cut off, these plants have a whole new look in winter to add another dimension to the winter garden. A bird swaying on top of a dried perennial plant in winter is such an amazing sight.

On the occasional icy morning, every twig and shrub will be outlined in icy transparency. Snow and ice somehow enhance the beauty of plants. Snow and frost on evergreens seem to show their every feature. Admittedly, too much of this can be hazardous for plants, but a little sure is pretty.

Take a few minutes to really look at the plants in the landscape this winter. While outside, enjoy the birds and other critters too. Take your camera. You'll be surprised what you will find.

White Barked Trees

Winter offers a great opportunity to see a tree's bark. Many trees offer spectacular bark. Too often people overlook this part of a plant's aesthetic qualities. But considering that most deciduous trees and shrubs are without leaves for many long winter months, we should consider using trees and shrubs with good bark character.

Some trees are actually more beautiful without foliage because of their bark. Good examples include *Acer griseum* and *Ulmus parvifolia*. *Acer griseum* goes by the common name of Paperbark Maple because of its spectacular bark, which is a cinnamon-brown that exfoliates to expose rich brown colors. *Ulmus parvifolia* is also called Lacebark Elm. It has magnificent bark with mottled combinations of gray, green, orange, and brown. Compared to other elms it shows considerable disease and insect resistance.

The trees most commonly planted for their bark characteristics are white-barked trees. Examples are birch, sycamore, and white poplars.

Paper birch trees are very popular, but unfortunately do not typically live long in central Illinois. Two commonly planted white birch trees are white birch (*Betula papyrifera*) and European White Birch (*Betula pendula*). Both have whitish bark, but the European's bark does not peel as much and with age the trunk becomes black. Both of these trees are extremely susceptible to the bronze birch borer. Therefore, I do not recommend planting these trees unless you are willing to replace them every few years.

A better option is to plant the white barked version of our native river birch (*Betula nigra* 'Heritage'). The Heritage River Birch is a patented selection introduced by Mr. Earl Cully from Jacksonville, Illinois. The bark on 'Heritage' peels on young trucks to a white or salmon-white and has superior vigor. Best of all the river birch is resistant to the bronze birch borer.

Sycamore trees are native trees with bark that exfoliates to a whitish color. This tree is one of the tallest of the native trees and commonly seen along streams and rivers. The American Sycamore (*Plantanus occidentalis*) grows 75 to 100 feet tall with a similar spread. It is great for naturalized plantings or as a single specimen (if you don't mind the nuisance fruit). This tree has creamy-colored bark compared to its relative the London Planetree (*Platanus* x *acerifolia*) that has more olive-colored bark.

White or Silver Poplars (*Populus alba*) have cream-colored bark. These are wide spreading, irregular shaped trees. Unfortunately, poplars are prone to many insect and disease problems and tend to be very messy; routinely dropping leaves, twigs, and branches. Therefore, poplars are not typically recommended as landscape trees.

Winter Gardening Activities

While on live local radio this month, I was asked what gardeners should do this time of the year. My response was read! Read gardening journals, magazines, catalogs, web sites, and more to prepare for summer gardens. I still think reading is the main February gardening activity, but here are some other activities for the winter gardener.

It is not too late to apply winter mulch, especially since there is no snow. You can apply mulch anytime after the ground is frozen. This practice supplements snow as an insulating blanket and prevents the ground from heaving due to alternate freezing and thawing. The feeding roots of many plants, especially perennials such as roses, are in the top 6 to 8 inches of soil. Soil heaving exposes these roots to air, so they dry and die, eventually causing twigs and branches to also die back.

Snow and ice can be quite destructive this month-if we get any. Remove heavy snow from low-growing shrubs such as Japanese yews or spreading junipers. Large amounts of snow can cause cracking and change the desirable form of valuable plants. The easiest method of removal is to gently tap the underside of the branches with a broom and let the snow sift down to the ground. If damage has already occurred, remove broken branches with a sharp pruning shear back to the point of breakage.

Although snow should be removed from shrubs, ice is a different story. Ice-coated branches will readily snap if they are struck to dislodge the ice. Although some trees and shrubs will lay flat to the ground from ice, they usually resume their normal shape after the ice naturally melts.

The best horticultural practice done this time of year is winter pruning. Most deciduous trees and shrubs really benefit from pruning done in winter. Most professionals agree that this is the best time of year to prune these plants. Scientifically it is better for the plants now and structurally you can see what you are doing better. For more information on how to properly prune trees and shrubs, contact your local Extension office.

You might consider attending a horticultural program or show this winter.

Other ideas for winter gardening include indoor herb gardens, houseplants, and starting seed indoors. Best of all enjoy the scenery. Winter offers a unique view of our beautiful plants. Like the weather, plants continually change throughout the year.

Winter Rose Care

Everyone loves roses! Roses are probably the most popular of all garden flowers. Growing roses requires some work, but they are definitely worth the trouble.

Basically, roses are separated into two main classes-bush roses and climbing roses. The bush roses are grouped into types according to their flowering habit, winter hardiness, and other traits and include hybrid tea, floribunda, wild, old fashioned, and the new carpet roses. The most commonly grown rose is the hybrid tea.

Regardless of the type of rose you have, most roses typically need winter protection in central Illinois. A key factor to successfully overwintering roses is maintaining a constant temperature around the plants. Winter protection is meant to keep the plants cold, not warm.

Do not plant or prune roses in the fall. Slight pruning may be necessary to accommodate some winter protection devices or to prevent winter winds from whipping the plants and loosening the root system. Additional pruning should be done in early spring when the winter protection is removed.

Do not cover your roses too early. Covering plants early, often before dormancy has been completed, is thought to be the major cause of winter rose death. In central Illinois, mid-to-late November is generally the time to apply winter protection for roses.

There are many different methods available to protect roses in the winter. For bush-type roses bushel baskets or commercial covers work well. Trim the canes back to fit underneath the cover. Secure the device with bricks or another heavy object so they won't blow away. Other ways of protecting the roses include leaves (oak work best), pine needles, straw, old sawdust, or bark chips. Depth of the material should be 12 inches. Soil is not recommended since it stays too wet and packs too much. In the spring, remove the cover or mulch and trim the canes back to healthy wood, just above the strong bud and thin the plants to 4 or 5 canes.

Climbing and rambling rose canes may also need winter protection. Lay the canes on a bed of straw and cover with more straw. Be sure to cover the crown. Keep the straw in place by tying it or covering it with a small amount of soil. In the spring, remove the covering, remove all damaged wood and place the canes or shoots back on the trellis. Since most climbing roses bloom on old wood, wait until after they bloom to do major pruning.

There are many sources of rose information. Check out the American Rose Society page at http://www.ars.org

Winterizing Containers

My new herb garden this year included two container-grown herbs: rosemary and laurel bay. I grew them in containers because they are not hardy here and need winter protection. Growing plants in containers is becoming very popular. Almost anything can be grown in containers, including trees and shrubs.

Unfortunately for those of us in central Illinois, containerized plants often experience severe winter injury and often death if unprotected. In containers, the roots of the plants are exposed to below-freezing temperatures on all sides. As temperatures fluctuate, the soil thaws and refreezes causing the plant to heave out of the soil. This tears the roots and can expose the roots to drying winds. Branches can be broken directly by strong winds or by the container tipping over. Sudden temperature changes can also damage the container itself causing it to crack.

Very large containers should weather fine without any extra protection. On the University of Illinois campus, the library used to have large containers (5 by 5 feet) with Amur Corktree in them. A container this large does not freeze solid, nor experience significant freezing and thawing action. Still, trees grown in containers only live, at best, 20 to 25 years.

Smaller containers will need extra protection. Small plants can easily be moved into a protected location such as a cool garage or basement. Temperatures should be in the upper 30's or lower 40's. Protecting large plants is a bigger challenge but it can be done. Covering the plant and the container thoroughly can help protect the plant. However, if the plant is too tender for our climate or if the winter is unusually harsh, these measures may not be adequate.

To aid in the success of the plant, select plants hardy for our area and make every effort to be sure the plant is going into the winter in a healthy state. Continue watering the plant through the fall. Do not fertilize after mid-summer. Woody plants should be encouraged to gradually cease growth and harden off in preparation for winter.

Since the real danger to these plants is from the frozen rootball, work to protect the root system. Wrap the container with burlap or straw to protect it. Some people will bury the entire container into the ground so that the ground can insulate it. Others will entirely encase the upper and lower plant in a "cage" of chicken wire stuffed with leaves or straw. Nurserymen often "mulch-in" container grown plants in the winter by lying them against each other and packing the container area with mulch.

Containerized trees and shrubs add a great deal to our landscapes. With proper winter protection, the same plant can provide beauty for many years.

LAST COLUMN

Farewell

It is difficult to write this week's column, as it is my last one. My official last day at University of Illinois Extension – Fulton County is January 16th. I am going to Springfield to serve as Associate Regional Director at Extension's West Central Regional office. It is with bittersweet feelings that I move on in my career. It is sad to leave you all, but I look forward to a new challenge which will allow me to use my education and experiences in a whole new way.

Over the past 8 ½ years, writing this column has been one of my favorite tasks. We have explored many horticultural topics together through this column and I have learned so much along the way.

Together we've explored lawn care, growing vegetables, flower maintenance, water gardens, and landscaping for wildlife. We learned about specific flowers including my favorites: lily-of-the-valley, poppies, jack-in-the-pulpit, and tropicals. We discovered new and old houseplants, such as Norfolk Island pine, Boston fern, Ti plant, Easter Lilies, and Poinsettias. We learned how to grow sprouts and herbs indoors and how to start seeds indoors in the spring. We now know where various "spirits" come from and more about spices, coffee, and sugar.

My favorite articles are the ones that discuss how plants help us live better and healthier lives. This is the message I leave you in my last column.

Plants are an essential part of our lives. They provide

oxygen for us to breath. They provide beauty and enhance our environment. They help relieve stress and provide psychological benefits. Gardening is a satisfying hobby. Research at the University of Illinois, NASA, and others prove the benefits of plants to humans.

Have you ever noticed how people choose seats next to plants when given a choice in malls or parks? Our world is busy and we are constantly bombarded with noise, movement, and chaos. Plants help relax us. Because of their simplicity, plants or natural scenes reduce physical and mental excitement and improve our health.

In my absence, University of Illinois Extension – Fulton County will continue to offer horticultural support for the residents of Fulton County. Inquiries are answered by a variety of educated personnel including 24 Master Gardeners and statewide Extension Educators and Specialists. The office has access to a digital diagnosis system. New to the county is Julia Pryor who will coordinate horticultural programs.

I look forward to working with the Fulton County Extension office in a new way as they "Put Knowledge to Work" in Fulton County. Happy Gardening!

Printed in the United States
91062LV00002B/103-198/A